I0134597

Molly III

The Untold Story

by

Rosemarie Smith

www.littlemolly.co.uk

Grosvenor House
Publishing Limited

This book is published by
Grosvenor House Publishing Ltd
Link House
140 The Broadway, Tolworth, Surrey, KT6 7HT.
www.grosvenorhousepublishing.co.uk

A CIP record for this book
is available from the British Library

ISBN 978-1-78623-296-0

Acknowledgements

My sincere thanks to:

Paul Butler (Detective Constable 1915 Public Protection Unit) Chesterfield Divisional HQ, Beetwell Street, Chesterfield, Derbyshire.

Lorna Anderson Police Woman (collar number 14021)

Mathew Lowe CPS Barrister

The Judge (Recorder)

Clive and Denise Powell, you gave me back my will to live, I thank you from the bottom of my heart.

Sally and all the staff at Trust House... and everyone who helped to bring justice after so many years of suffering, I cannot express how much that means to me, many thanks!

Who Am I?

I am the epitome of everything feminine. My strength, resilience and determination are unmatched.

I uplift those who are downtrodden, strengthen those who are weak and guide those who are lost.

I have enough experience and have 'overcome' enough struggles to do so!

I am the one person who people can look up to when they are in a mess... to help them through it!

I will help those who have wronged me, because at the end of it all... it is not what people deserve but what I believe in!

I am 'A Survivor'.

This book is dedicated to all those who have and still are suffering from abuse; too frightened to come forward.

My thoughts are with you.

Foreword

This is the story of success in its own right; when justice prevails!

Over a period of several years, the author, Rosemarie Smith wrote her autobiography in three separate books, *Little Molly*, *Molly II (Am I Who I Should Be)* and now, *Molly III (The Untold Story)* but because of the seriousness of the abuse that her brother inflicted upon her, she struggled to give a hundred per cent account of the hurt, pain and damage she suffered as a result of it. Having suffered the consequences of several breakdowns she reached a point where she had totally given up on life and felt that the long hard battle to survive just wasn't worth the pain anymore. In *Molly III (The Untold Story)* she gives her own account of what it was like growing up, suffering severe, physical and mental abuse; and then to go on suffering most of her life. Just as she had given up on society and every government body, came a massive break-through when she received a message from Paul Butler, a police officer from the Chesterfield Divisional Head Quarters, Beetwell Street, Derbyshire. And as a result of a short conversation over the telephone, on July 12 2017 a judge (recorder) ruled 'life in prison' for her childhood abuser and said, "Rosemarie Smith's 'statement of facts' was so compelling." He believed that the abuser,

John Wass, had committed every sexual and indecent act that his victims gave evidence on. It took fifty years to bring this case to court but Rosemarie said, "It is never too late to report abuse!"

Prologue

Many things have happened since I wrote *Little Molly* and *Molly II (Am I Who I Should Be?)* including the beginning of this book, but after spending almost four years writing and then putting it off, I have decided it is time to bring this part of my life to closure as I no longer feel it is necessary to make all my life public; so on Saturday 28 January 2017 I began to write what I believe will be the book before 'A New Beginning'.

I see life as a learning curve, many things happen that are out of our control and we tend to blame ourselves for things that go wrong in our lives. My life especially has not been a happy one, although I cannot say I have been miserable or unhappy all of the time as I can still remember the happiest moments of my life bringing me so much more happiness than I ever thought possible. And so I begin 'The Trilogy' to *Little Molly*, recalling the moments of my life, way back in the days when I was a little girl and the only thing that ever seemed to matter to me was bread and butter and daisy chains.

Coming from a large poor family we didn't have many toys to play with, although I do still remember what I would now term as, 'A Poor Man's Christmas'! My mother and father were both Christians and as far as I know had equal belief in the Bible, so Christmas was focussed upon the Nativity. Although my memory of such times is now very limited, I still remember the plastic nativity scene they displayed alongside our small Christmas tree, each and every year, when I learned that baby Jesus, Joseph and Mary were part and parcel of our Christian belief and was considered the norm. Our Christmas tree and decorations were never flamboyant, and Mother could never afford to go over the top buying in all the traditional food and treats for everyone, but being one of the youngest of our family, I fitted into the category of children who still believed in Father Christmas; so, I received a very modest number of toys and sweets on Christmas Day. I loved Christmas, and although there were times when Mother and Father could not afford to buy coal to heat the water and keep us warm, I remember we all seemed happy and content. I remember there were times when we all seemed to appreciate and protect each other, being the seventh child born to my parents it seemed I had no problem acquiring protection from my older siblings; but one day my whole world came crashing down and everything changed…

—◊◊—

A conversation with Kim Briggs on Facebook gave me the incentive to write *Molly III (the Untold Story)*. I recall I was chatting with my sister Julia at the time, when it was bought to my attention that a twenty-one-year-old had said she had recently married a member of my family and had the audacity to send me several requests to add her to my friends list. At that particular time, I had no idea who she was or how she had come across my profile. I had very few friends, and apart from my sister Julia and my immediate family I had very limited contacts. As the days passed, I found that the man she was referring to was my abuser, my brother, John Wass. I was absolutely astounded, so totally ignored her requests. I was certain I didn't know her, and I wasn't interested in getting to know her; although she seemed insistent. Eventually she made it common knowledge that she was having a relationship with him and considered herself to be part of our family and began to contact other family members as well as myself. As always, with the slightest connection to my brother, fear was my first emotion. I surmised she had already read *Little Molly*, part one of my autobiographies and I believed, as I still do now, that she was aware of John Wass's paedophilic record. She did not use our family name and although I could understand why she wouldn't want to, I surmised she was lying when she actually said she had married him. What I failed to understand was how she could associate herself with the likes of him, knowing he could never be trusted around anyone's children; and why she would want to get in touch with me. John had always been a violent bully and I spent my whole life trying to avoid him or anyone he associated with, so I asked myself, why me?

When I first decided to write my autobiography, the thought of reliving my abusive childhood frightened the hell out of me, although I had toyed with the thought that maybe one day I might develop the courage to write something about it – for many years I was reluctant. I didn't really want to drag my siblings through that painstaking journey again, recalling all the heartache and suffering we all went through, so initially I opted for what I thought would be easiest and contemplated writing a poetry book instead, but then I thought long and hard about other small children who might have been suffering; and like a gift from God I was given the incentive to write the first part of my autobiography, *Little Molly*, hoping it would help all those who had suffered; and those who are still suffering. So here I am once again on a warm September evening in the year 2010; hoping that continuing my story will help all who read it.

Author's Notes

When I first began to write I had no idea that I would spend the best part of seven years reliving the terrible abuse and neglect I suffered as a child. But in the short time it took me to write *Little Molly* and *Molly II* I felt I had crossed bridges that I was once too frightened to cross and came to terms with everything that had happened to me; and I accepted that 'life goes on!'.

I recall, when my counsellor, Clive Powell, first challenged me into writing *Little Molly* I thought it was a ludicrous idea. I was just recovering from what I believed was a nervous breakdown, but as time moved on it seemed more apparent that it was a, complete physical breakdown; and the very slow and painful recovery began almost as soon as I met him. The breakdown had such an effect on my life that it crippled me mentally and I could barely function, but within that first year of intensive counselling I had pieced together some of my most horrific childhood memories and managed to build the foundation of *Little Molly*; the first part of my autobiography. However, even on completion of *Little Molly* I knew I had so much more to tell, so went on to write *Molly II (Am I Who I Should Be?)*. Now I realise that even after completing two 'Molly' books; there is still an endless amount untold, so I continue to write *Molly III (The Untold Story)*.

Some of the names in this book have been changed in order to protect the innocent. As with *Little Molly* and *Molly II*, I have decided to omit certain memories for the sake of my family. If, however, I have offended anyone, I apologise most sincerely.

Rosemarie Smith

A Letter to My Brother

Honestly, facing up to you was the most difficult thing I had ever done, but it was worth it, for me, my children and others too. You hurt me so bad, killed my trust and you changed me. I never thought I would grow strong enough but despite the odds, I did it! I am the only one who knows how much pain you caused me and how difficult my life has been because of you, but I am healing. As I look back on my life I realise that every time I thought I had everything to live for, you showed up and broke me. I was always determined you would never do to my children what you had always done to me and continued doing; without ever thinking how much pain and suffering you caused. I won't look back; I am at peace with myself.

One thing you never really understood, I was your sister! A little girl who could have grown to be your friend, you could have trusted me, confided in me and learned from me, but when you made the choice to become my abuser, you not only destroyed me, but yourself too! You destroyed the one and only person who could have possibly helped you to return to normality, helped you to return to a man with a healthy mental balance, rationality; but you made your choices. I probably know you well enough to know what you are thinking right now, that we, your victims, are responsible for you going to prison, but we're not; you are!

Contents

CONTENTS

CHAPTER 1

Remembering the Past

When I was a child I found it impossible to tell anyone about the pain and suffering my abuser caused me, I was just a tiny little girl and, although he was my brother, he was a man capable of lies and deception, therefore he found it easy to convince my peers that what little vocabulary I had was nothing more than a few words of a young child's distorted imagination. I will never forget when he desperately tried to convince the police that it was my father who abused me, had I not been old enough to validate the truth he would have walked away scot-free. During my communication with Kim Briggs, she informed me that she wasn't interested in anything John Wass had done before she had met him and that his past was his past; but I sensed uncertainty in the way she drafted her messages, as she tried to convince me he wasn't the paedophile I knew him to be. As I tried to convince her of the truth, I cleared my mind of the pain and suffering that he had caused me but many of the abusive images invaded my thoughts as I explained to her what it felt like to be a four-year-old child suffering at the hands of a paedophile. Then I asked myself; did she really know what she had let herself in for? With so many hidden secrets, it would have taken her a lifetime to know my brother, John Wass, like I did.

I once asked my sister, Carol, why she referred to me as 'Sad eyes'; a nickname I remembered from the past. I didn't like the name and although it seemed self-explanatory, just to make her feel as bad as I felt each time she referred to it, I asked her to verify her reasons for calling me such a name, but it didn't seem to faze her; but then nothing did. I think one of the worst things about growing up around Carol was the fact that she held so much knowledge of the abuse I had suffered, and often found it necessary to inform friends of hers when we were both out socialising, not really understanding how I felt about it. All I wanted was to forget about John Wass and what he had done to me and live in peace; but as she repeatedly told her version of what had happened when we all lived as a family I held back my tears, so I didn't look weak. I didn't want anyone to think I was vulnerable, so I put up this hard exterior pretending it no longer bothered me but that only seemed to provoke her into telling more, she seemed to find it difficult not to bring it into a conversation when I was with her and although I am certain it wasn't something she did purposely, she placed so much doubt and uncertainty into people's minds about me. Occasionally, I built up enough courage to protest and tried to evade the painful questions that her friends asked me about the memories I had been storing inside my head for years. When I think back and remember all the devastating things I had suffered, I realise it was not just the effects of the abuse I carried with me, but also the degradation of the terrifying medical examinations that followed it. It was something I had never released from my thoughts and yet it was one of the most horrifying memories I had. I still remember the couch where I was laid and the array of silver instruments which had been neatly organised and put on top of the trolley in full view of me. The oversized stirrups, which were normally used to examine pregnant women, literally frightened the hell out of me as they were casually unfolded and erected around each of my thighs – their purpose to take the strain as my legs were held apart, while being examined internally. No steps were taken to lessen my embarrassment and no sheet to keep me warm or comfort me; an ordeal that constantly reminded me of the terrible trauma of the abuse John Wass had inflicted upon me. I cannot recall how many times I had wished I had never been born, but as I sit at my desk I try to forget everything he ever did to me, and to remember some of the happier moments I experienced; I try to clear my mind of Kim Briggs and I wonder... where do I begin?

For me the beginning always seems to be the hardest part and yet, once I have finally found the right place, a torrent of words flow; as memories flood in from the past...

I woke up this morning thinking about all the years I had spent in the children's homes and wondered how on earth I had survived. When I was removed from my family home at the age of nine I was taken to live at Springhill Children's Home which was referred to as 'a reception placement' which was situated in Duffield, in Derby where I felt really happy and settled. But then I was removed, along with two of my younger siblings, and was taken to live at the Outrake Children's Home which was situated in the Peak District, a tiny village called Little Longstone where I lived alongside twenty or so other children and slowly developed into a teenager. This was where I spent hour upon hour, day after day with other unfortunate children, who like myself endeavoured to pass time composing letters to our parents who we barely ever saw, only to witness the staff screw the letters up into the palms of their hands and dispose of them soon after. I recall there were times when I tried to write poetry, but my mind focussed on nothing else but the abuse I had suffered, so I doodled and scribbled onto pieces of paper that I carelessly tore out of my school books and received punishment for when I returned to school. Desperate to try and prevent my abusive childhood from destroying my future, I tried to bury the memories that taunted me and built a barrier so tough around myself that I allowed no one to pass through it; or get close to me. I suffered in silence, hoping to forget everything that had ever happened to me, but I just couldn't rid myself of the past.

So many bad memories to counteract the good and yet the power of determination overrides everything; and I am able to continue my story.

The Outrake, now better known as Chestnut House, is situated on the edge of the Peak District at Little Longstone, Derbyshire; where I lived for just a small part of my life. After many years of wondering what was going to happen to the oversized mansion, I found myself returning to it and staying in one of the little cottages that it had been divided into. The Outrake's kitchen had become Chatsworth Cottage with its large, wrought iron spiral staircase that dominated the open plan living area and led up to the twin bedroom which used to be the boys' dormitory before it was assigned to the girls. When I met Annie, the proprietor of Chestnut

House, my first response when she opened the door was one of shock to see how much they had altered what I will always remember as the Outrake Children's Home. Although I tried to look and sound pleased with the alterations, and the presence of the large spiral staircase to the left of me, I could have cried a mountain of tears. I felt so full of emotion I couldn't speak and didn't really understand why I felt that way, apart from the Outrake's old cook, Connie, I only visualised myself and my friend Shirley standing at the old kitchen sink, way back when we were children, peeling so many potatoes – I learned to hate that job. I suppose I expected to walk inside and find everything the same as I had left it when I was a child. Remembering it was my first permanent home, I recalled the day I was removed from my own family home by the Derbyshire Social Services in 1966, the year my whole family was divided; and I began the journey of a lifetime. I was nine years old when I arrived at the Outrake Children's Home and it looked so daunting, the very thought of entering the house put tremendous fear into my bones, I was crying for what seemed an age and even after many weeks of being there, I still cried myself to sleep at night.

My younger siblings seemed much braver than me, although I often caught them standing in a corner all alone; crying a mountain of tears. I reassured them with words and promises I knew I couldn't fulfil but I felt it was something that was expected of me; being their older sister and all. We had been through so much and come so far, I desperately hoped that the Outrake would be the fairy-tale ending to our dreams, hopes and wishes; I didn't want to believe we were put on this earth just to suffer; and so, I raised my guard one more time knowing we weren't going to have an easy time of it. There was no feeling of belonging, no responsible parent to take care of us and no trusting family member to rely on, we were on our own. Three unruly, vulnerable children left to the mercy of those who really didn't want to take care of us, so all we could do was follow the instructions and commands of those who were going to spend years moulding us into the type of children that deserved to live inside an Edwardian mansion. As a vulnerable child fear engulfed me, and I felt sick inside, little thoughts ran through my mind as I entered the large house for the very first time and I wondered, why u s, why couldn't we have been born in another time, different place, different world? It seemed so unfair!

As I stood staring at the spiral staircase, I realised that memories were all I had left of my childhood and the beautiful mansion that was once my home had been altered; but not beyond recognition! As I looked around the room I stood up in, I still recognised it as the kitchen that I worked all those long hours in and felt kind of restricted by the blocked doorways and locked cupboards that I used to have access to when I was a child. I wondered what the rest of the house was like, whether it had been changed beyond recognition or was it like the old kitchen that still had the tell-tale signs of a children's care home that was well and truly imprinted inside my mind. Although a big part of me felt saddened that the place had been altered; a small part of me felt pleased that something of it still remained.

—ᴍ—

CHAPTER 2

The Promise I Made

I seldom think back to my childhood days but today my mind drifted back to the time when I was really happy and enjoyed being part of a family. Having nine other siblings proved difficult most of the time but there were occasions when we all enjoyed normal, family play; bouncing on our beds was a favourite pastime and just like every other child we enjoyed the occasional pillow fight. I recall the day, me and my siblings tried to re-enact the story of Little Red Riding Hood – it was a regular pastime for me and my older brother, Trevor, and occasionally our younger siblings joined in to make up the four main characters. Sometimes, I find it impossible to recall all the laughter, fun and games we played when our family seemed relatively normal; but I do remember building a close bond between many of my siblings. Up until the separation of our parents everything was typical of a poor man's family, surviving the best way they could, and if we ever complained, Mother and Father told us repeatedly that one day we would look back on our lives and wish we could live it all over again. Of course, that was partly true, although at that time I am sure they were both unaware of the abuse I was suffering. I try to focus solely on the good times we had and pretend the abuse didn't happen, but I feel my hurt and sadness is permanently fixed at the forefront of my mind and sometimes, I think of nothing else but that! Then I realise somewhere inside my head, the memories of all the good times I experienced are being preserved and remain at the back of my mind and so I wonder; when will I remember them?

My mind drifts and I think of my own childrens' lives and try to compare theirs against mine. I would like to say I had a similar upbringing to my own children, with family outings, bike rides and hot meals served around the table; with food enough to feed extra mouths of friends they invited. I would like to say I was loved and well cared for and bathed every night before being tucked into bed with blankets and quilts that kept me warm and snug. I would like to say there was always someone there when I fell and grazed my knee or cut my hand while rummaging for food; but of course, that wasn't the kind of life I experienced. My life was different; it was nothing like my children's lives, so it cannot be compared with theirs! As I sit and mull over the awful remarks that some people have made about me, I wonder if it would ever be possible to put into words the difference between my upbringing and theirs. I wonder if I will ever know enough about English literature to enable me to describe in the best possible way, how much better their life was to mine… Maybe, maybe not! I never wanted my children to know how tough my childhood had been, but when people who didn't really know me intervened and remarked on things they knew nothing about, I found it necessary to be more upfront with them; one of the reasons I felt it necessary to write my autobiography! After writing *Little Molly* and *Molly II*, I promised my daughter, Cheniel, that I would try and recall some of the good things my mother did with her life before the breakup of our family; as I know only too well that sometimes bad memories overpower the good and they are all I remember… and so I begin *Molly III* remembering the day that my brother, Simon, was born.

I came in from school not expecting Mother to be home as I had already gotten used to not seeing her around so much, her fingers were raw to the bone from working all the hours at the factory, she referred to as, 'Potters'; a place that lived up to its name and produced lots of earthenware – pottery made of baked clay. She had worked for many years, all through her married life and before, at Pearson's, Robinsons, and other factories situated in and around Chesterfield; the town where I was born. The work that took place inside the factories was gruelling, in those days there was no easy way of earning a living, but she was a good employee and worked really hard to keep her job; despite the pain it caused her. Having suffered from diphtheria, an acute infectious disease caused by the Klebs-Loffler bacillus, as a small child, she suffered lots of side effects and was left crippled and remained in callipers until the age of fourteen; so, her life proved to be very difficult at times. The constant pain that she suffered in her legs was one of the lesser side effects, but it didn't deter her from working. I recall whenever she spoke to me about her own childhood and suffering from a form of paralysis caused by the diphtheria, she never complained much and always seemed grateful that she had lived through the war and was able to lead a relatively normal life. She told me there was no vaccine against diphtheria in those days and she was one of the very few who had suffered; but survived it!

The 17th of April 1966, I was seven years old and as I arrived home from school I ran through the front door of our house, not expecting to see Mother there but as I ran into the kitchen I recall her sitting at the table on one of the very few chairs we had, she looked tired and wan and was nursing a baby in what seemed a bundle of clothing. My eldest sister Anne, who was aged twenty at the time, stood in front of her, and my older sister, Carol, was leant against the dining room door; a little behind her. They were speaking in very low-key voices and looking down at the newborn baby that Mother held in her arms. He was dressed all in white and looked so clean I was frightened to touch him for fear my grubby fingers would tarnish his matinee coat. His dark hair and his beautiful olive coloured skin made him the most beautiful baby I had ever seen. After taking stock of his tiny fingers and his little button nose I asked with excitement, "Mam, whose is it? Whose is it Mam?"

"Shush, Molly! Shush! You'll wake him," she said in her broad Derbyshire accent.

"But, Mam, whose is it?" I asked. "Is it ours?"

"Course its fuckin' ours, whose du yur think it is? Shift, get away from him," Carol snarled as she looked across at me.

Paying very little attention to or her sarcasm, I excitedly asked, "Can I hold it, Mam? Can I? Can I?" I repeatedly asked.

Suddenly, and without so much as a word, she very slowly and lovingly placed the little bundle into my arms, while she kept a gentle hold of him. I nursed him only for a few seconds but within that time I had taken stock of everything about him, the clean fresh smell that lingered about his clothing, his little white socks and the colour of his ebony hair. "What's its name, Mam?" I asked quietly.

"Simon," she uttered. "His name is Simon."

As I put my arms around him I felt the warmth of his skin on my hands and as I gently patted the bundle, just like Mother did, he won my heart instantly. As I listened to Mother, Anne and Carol talking, I looked down at him and felt my heart miss a beat, as I suddenly realised he was my baby brother. I was so excited, I couldn't wait to tell my friends. As Mother gently prized him from my arms, I reluctantly let go; but waited anxiously for another chance to hold him before I ran outside to tell everyone that I had a new baby brother.

Each and every one of us took turns to hold Simon that day and literally pleaded with Mother again and again to allow us to hold him some more, until she was so worn down that she put a stop to our nonstop pestering and placed him into his pram to sleep. It was one of those moments when Mother's patience seemed to be everlasting and I and my siblings changed when we realised we could not fight and argue like we used to; but tiptoed around the house so as not to wake him. As I desperately try to recall the happier moments of my life, I realise even memories I hold closest to my heart are tainted with all the hardship and abuse I suffered as a child but, for the sake of my children I delve to the back of my mind, trying to decipher the good from the bad so I can record the happier moments of my childhood.

Up until the moment of writing my first book 'Little Molly' all I could think about was the abuse and neglect I had suffered, but now I feel I owe it to my parents, as well as my children, to record some of the better moments of my life. Although I seem to remember very few moments when I felt as happy as I did when Simon was born; it seemed even then it was just the simple things that made me happy. I recall the very first time I ever noticed, that a combination of stars amalgamated above my head and brightened the darkened sky; as I roamed the streets at night. I was around eight years old and had suddenly learned that part of my education included a weekly visit to the school library van and books seemed to play a significant part of school life. Although I was far less able to read than most, I found looking through a book, observing pictures gave me hours of enjoyment and I loved it. But the ridicule I encountered from other children, when it became obvious I could not comprehend the art of reading, I became a target and was picked on by children who were far more able; it was at that time of my life I became unsociable and withdrew from the class. My teacher, Miss Chalmers, was a pleasant character, tall and slim with a hint of orient about her, however I pushed her patience when, through no fault of my own, I regularly failed to attend school and became the typical outcast, whose lack of punctuality and unruly behaviour not only put me at the bottom of the class academically but also at the lower end of her estimation. Although I originally enjoyed school it took only a few months for me to fear the high expectations the teacher had of me, so just like my siblings I began to hate school. I lived solely by my family's rules and because I was just a small child it was impossible for me to counteract what they impelled. It felt natural to submerge myself into *The Giant Book of Old Mother Goose Stories* that I yearned to read like the other children; yet my lack of concentration interfered with everything I did so I failed drastically. It was only because of my family's love of music that I discovered many of the songs they sang I committed to memory and learned them off by heart. 'Twinkle! Twinkle! Little Star' was one of the first songs I ever learned to sing but even so, the continual chanting of such songs did not increase my knowledge of the night sky or indeed our universe. The colossal formation of beautiful stars in the sky did not enter into my world, until my family considered me old enough to run after-dark errands for my mother. Although I cannot be entirely certain of my age at that time, I recall that I marvelled at the alluring night sky, as I realised for the very first time that the North Star we spoke about in class was not just part of an advent story we re-enact every year at Yuletide; but was actually an incredible part of our world.

—m—

CHAPTER 3

Our Family Life

I recall, I was around four years old, it was a hot summer's day and I had just been bathed in the old porcelain sink, which was situated between two highly scrubbed, wooden draining boards, in what was probably the busiest part of our kitchen. My younger siblings had already been bathed and dressed and waited anxiously for me to be dried and dressed before we were allowed to join the older siblings in the waiting process, before the whole family left our house dressed in their Sunday best. An outing to 'The Foxen Dam' was enjoyed by all and caused an infectious pattern of excitement. It was quite a distance from our house but a place we all loved so much we giggled and chattered excitably as we made our way around the estate; we loved to go there. Bluebells adorned the woods with their magnificent array of colour and many other families enjoyed picnics at the water's edge; it was a lovely feeling walking out with my parents when our family was together. They hadn't separated then, and their troubles seemed very few and far between. All my siblings seemed reasonably happy and, apart from John dominating the whole family, we all seemed to care a little for each other. Mother and Father showed us how to cut through our estate and down water-pitted lanes to arrive at the 'Foxen Dam' much quicker than we would have done had we walked all the way around the main roads. By the time we had arrived there it seemed like we had been walking most of the day and for miles, but as soon as we caught site of the water's edge we ran through the woods screaming with delight; calling out to each other as we trailed carelessly through the carpet of blue-bells and bracken. We ran and skimmed stones across the water's edge and picked bluebells by the armful. Mother and Father allowed us to paddle in the shallow end of the dam and watched caringly as the water rippled silently around our feet, I loved the water and the warm sun-shine. I watched the sun's rays as it glistened through the tree tops and listened to the shrill of the birds that echoed all around me. My older siblings produced a variety of warbling sounds with simple blades of grass that they had picked from beneath the bluebells. It was the perfect place where we roamed freely, and yet I felt such a strong sense of security where I was at my happiest; family life was pretty good back then! I had begun to attend Eckington Pimary School despite the fact that Mother hadn't really wanted me to, apart from one other child I was the youngest in the class. I remember the heated conversations that Mother had with the authorities before she had agreed to let me go, simply because she had considered me too young to attend and begged them to allow me to stay at home for just another year... but I attended anyway. Mother was no different from any other mother at that time, she developed such a strong bond with us that wild horses would not have torn her away from us, and she shed a mountain of tears as each and every one of us slowly reached school age and entered the big wide world of education. By the time

I had started school my older siblings, Anne and John, had already left school and were working, but Julia, Carol, David and Trevor were at varying levels of their educational years and attended school just like everyone else. Trevor of course was a year older than me, so we schooled closely together which left Andrew and Lorraine at home as they were far too young to attend school; so remained at home with Mother. I consider those early school days to be some of the happiest days of my life, when I tasted my very first rich tea biscuit and lost my first milk tooth eating it. Losing a tooth back then was never treated as a great trauma but considered as part of our natural development, something we were taught to expect but I still remember sitting crossed legged on the parker knoll flooring in the school hall crying about it, as I hadn't expected to lose any teeth on my first day at school. But I was the happiest child alive when I found a shiny new penny beneath my pillow the following morning; a gift from the fairies in exchange for my tooth I was told… I believed that story right up until I was age twelve.

The memories I have of my earliest school days, although very vague, are some of the happiest memories I have of my childhood. The aroma of the freshly cut grass immediately springs to mind as I recall the beautiful hot summers that we had back then and the trailing daisy chains that I learned to make while playing with other children. The uneven, giant, playing field was the recreational ground that supplied lots of entertainment for me and many other children that used the hills to roly-poly down during break times. And the masses of buttercups we picked and used to prove, with a hint of reflection beneath our chins, that every one of us loved butter; an old wives tale that was told for many years, but I believed it anyway! Eckington Primary was a lovely school, although I experienced first day nerves and like the varied few, wet my pants – as I had just turned four and proved to be a very nervous child. I recall, I sat rigid on the highly buffed flooring in a pool of urine just waiting for someone to notice me, too frightened to move or raise my hand as the headmistress had suggested when I first entered the room. Listening to the headmistress's instructions on how to get to our classroom from the main hall and to the children's toilets took far too long and, before I knew it, I had embarrassed myself; I was absolutely heartbroken. My freshly laundered dress and pants were soaked and I hung my head with shame and embarrassment as my new teacher led me through the hall and out of the main entrance into the car park while every other child remained crossed legged and seated on the hall floor. The best thing I remember about that day was that I was taken home in my teacher's car; she was really kind and experienced enough to know about a young girl's pride and tried to play the incident down; while explaining to my mother what had happened. I felt traumatised by the whole thing, but I was soon put at ease and returned to school in shorts and a tee-shirt; ready to start the day. I recall Mother enduring difficulties calmly in those days and seemingly had lots of patience, she was happy to have us around then and nothing seemed too much trouble for her, although we were high spirited and downright rowdy at times, she kept her cool and made difficult tasks look simple. I remember there being many times when she was without a washing machine and used a dolly tub to wash all our clothes in and regularly exert herself trying to remove stubborn stains with the smallest piece of dark green Fairy washing soap, which she sliced from a long cake of soap that she bought from the tiny hardware shop opposite our house. Life was difficult for our parents at that time, it was just after the war and our country had suffered massively. Food was scarce and butter, milk, cheese and eggs where rationed and meat was considered a luxury that many families went without. I'm sure we would have starved had Dad not grown his own vegetables! My mother told me that my grandmother made a lot of my siblings' clothing which was continually passed down from the eldest to the youngest, until they outgrew them, then each garment was taken apart and re-made to fit us younger ones; it was the way most families survived back then.

I don't remember my grandmother, as I am told I was only aged two when she died, and it wasn't until the coroner carried out a post-mortem on her that they found that she suffered from cancer at the base of her spine; which explained many undiagnosed symptoms that she had suffered from. I rely only on the stories that my siblings and my cousin Norman tell of her, according to them she was a very fine woman who spent most of her time caring for other people. Mother spoke highly of her and made it known to me that she loved her very dearly, she was someone Mother could rely on, she was her spirit, her backbone but when she died I think part of Mother died too as it was then that our mother suffered her first breakdown; that was when our family began to suffer. Mourning for two whole years, Mother desperately tried to keep the family together, while she struggled to get over the death of her beloved mother, but it was all too much for her and our lives just gradually fell apart; as she never recuperated. Over a period of six years, Mother suffered two breakdowns and terrible bouts of depression that she couldn't shake off. Her life became so unmanageable that she found it impossible to cope with managing our home and after many cries for help, eventually abandoned us, not thinking about the consequences. Subsequently, we were removed from our family home and placed into the care of the Derbyshire Social Services Department. I was nine years old at the time and couldn't understand why my whole world had fallen apart. My brother John Wass had been released from prison after serving a few years for what was termed as a 'taken into account (TIC)'... The punishment he received for sexually abusing me. I was aged six when he went to prison but it's only recently that I learned he had committed a burglary at the same time so his charges for the sexual offences were taken as a TIC alongside the burglary, which lessened the time he served in prison; I was absolutely astounded by that information. He had been in and out of trouble with the police most of his life and, I recall, he had been sexually and physically abusing me most of mine, so what upsets me now is not the fact that I had been taken into care for abandonment and neglect but the fact that John Wass got away so lightly with abusing me. In less than four years he was returned to our family home by the probation service which was instrumental in getting him put into prison in the first place. The probation service and the social services department allowed him to gain access to me and left me at his mercy all over again, that's when I became his victim again! Mother suffered greatly when she lost her mother and then the trauma of a broken marriage was all too much for her to bear, so I watched her keel over, heartbroken! Yet still I couldn't understand why she had abandoned us; knowing the devastation she once felt when Father left.

I recall the day my father died, he had been divorced from my mother for many years by then but, when I went to break the news of his death to her I didn't find it easy; despite the terrible trauma they had caused us. My heart sank as I entered her home. What I wanted to do was bawl her out for not being there for him and curse the day she divorced him, but I couldn't. Instead, I stood in front of her and cried like I had never cried before, not expecting her to be moved or shaken by it; as I had only ever seen her cry during moments of hardship when I was just a little girl. I recall I stood in the middle of her living room, feeling so much sorrow it felt like my whole world had crumbled around me. I don't exactly recall what I said to her but as usual she controlled her emotions and remained poised for some time before it all got too much for her, and then she broke down, it was like the whole heavens had opened up and her tears flowed freely to the ground; she was absolutely heartbroken. She repeatedly said that she had always loved him; and a part of her loved him still... but I already knew that!

—⁂—

❦ Chapter 4 ❦

Casting my Mind Back

I recall December 1972; I was fourteen years old and had just been returned to my mother after spending almost five years in the care homes. The thing I had wanted most in the world was to be returned to her, but when I was we quarrelled regularly and couldn't see eye to eye. I blamed her for everything that had happened in the past and could not see how life had been for her. Nobody took any responsibility for the ruin of our family and because she was my mother I assumed the entire blame lay with her. When me and my siblings were taken into care we were separated and passed from one children's home to another and I had never considered anyone to blame for that but her; but now I realise that my father was jointly responsible for our welfare and, although he was ill, I think he could have done more to help her. I also understand now how difficult it must have been for her to accept that her first born son had sexually abused me, he is my oldest brother; what a cruel blow that must have been for her! I could not begin to imagine how I would have felt had that happened to me or my children. She was our mother and I suppose she felt as much love for John as she did for me and felt she couldn't choose between us;

I suppose it was that which finally broke her. Now I've had time to reflect, I realise that it wasn't Mother's fault that John sexually abused me! He was responsible for his own actions but because the police, the social services and every other authoritative individual blamed Mother, I feel because of that, John considered he was innocent and went on to abuse many others. He continued to make excuses for his behaviour and blamed innocent people for his own wrongdoings. Over many years he regularly informed members of my family that it was me that had abused him and told them that I wouldn't leave him alone; I sometimes wondered if he really believed that! He occasionally accused my sisters of the same and described unbelievable episodes of rape and group sexual activities that he said they had taken part in. Because I was convinced he had severe psychological problems, when I was old enough to converse, I occasionally informed Mother of the allegations he so regularly made; but it seemed she just didn't know what to make of it all. He had caused so much heartache and mistrust amongst us all; none of us really knew whom or what to believe. I described to my sister Carol phone calls that he had made to my home, after he obtained my phone number from another member of the family and although I regret it now, on one occasion I even persuaded her to endure the awful experience through the loudspeakers; knowing that hearing was believing. But she could not bear to listen to the disgusting accusations he made about her and my older sisters, unable to endure the pain of listening to his very descriptive sexual episodes of abuse, she left the room in tears, halfway through his one-sided conversation. Had I not known him better, his very convincing manner would have even put doubt into my own mind about my sisters, but I had suffered at the hands of this man all my life and knew, apart from everything else, he was a compulsive liar! Since I became an adult I have realised he got off on our fear and embarrassment and had mastered the art of convincing each and every one of us that, following a short spell in prison he had finally learnt his lesson and would never be a threat to us again but, he knew, and I knew, that was a lie too! It was ironic really; even after all the years of trying to convince my family of the terrible things he had done, there was always the varied few who doubted my word – until something happened to them!

The problem was, because this type of thing seemed to happen more often back then, many of us thought it was a natural part of growing up; and many are still convinced of that! When I was in my teens, I was never able to convince my family that he was as dangerous as I had described and was often told by particular members, "You should have stopped him abusing you when you were young; then he wouldn't have carried on abusing you!" I remember thinking, what did they know? They were so naïve and didn't understand what he was capable of. Then one day out of the blue, screams penetrated the walls of my mother's house and could be heard by all, but it was too late, even with a house full of guests he had managed to single out and trap the most vulnerable of us inside Mother's kitchen; to masturbate in front of them before anyone could stop him… John began to abuse me well before my fourth birthday, I was just a baby, too young to resist his attacks; what defence did I have? I recall; as a young woman I had no one to turn to and nowhere to call home as he continually stalked me and threatened my very existence. He regularly approached me and masturbated in front of me. He had mentally scarred me, and I feared him so much I daren't report him to the police again. I had tried to convince the authorities so many times, throughout the whole of my life but I accepted it was just a waste of time and effort trying to get them to do something about him. I felt like I was the only person in the world, so alone that my only wish was to cease to exist; knowing that the pain and fear would only stop if I was no longer a part of this world.

Thursday 6 January 2014, I am drawn to my sister Julia's wall on Facebook where a message has been left by my brother John, he overtly informs everyone that he has recently made contact with someone he hasn't seen for a while. I was sickened by the comments left by unsuspecting people congratulating him and saying how nice it was for him to see her again. Of course, they were unaware of his past history, when he was banned from living with children or even having contact with them. My heart goes out to her; for I fear she may not know him. I don't only fear for her safety but for any children she may have had. I wonder if anyone has informed her of his paedophilic tendencies... I suspect not. For reasons I cannot understand, family have thoughtlessly brushed his criminal record and paedophilic tendencies aside and remained silent; fearful it may bring retribution for him. But now I face my fears and accept that, although he is capable of doing any-thing, I will do my utmost to protect the innocent from him; despite his previous threats to harm me. Before

I wrote *Little Molly* I had considered writing many things, a children's adventure story book, a cook book and even a poetry book but, no matter what I put my mind to my thoughts reverted back to the abuse that I had suffered and my very unhappy childhood; so, I found it impossible to concentrate on anything else. Then I remembered my counsellor saying, "You could write your autobiography."

But I asked him, "What could I write about? Apart from having my children and the terrible life I have lived; I have nothing nice to write."

Then Clive's words ran repeatedly through my head, "Buy yourself a nice thick notebook and pen, pick a nice quiet spot in your house and write the first thing that enters your mind!" He made it sound so easy, so I chose the quietest room at the back of my house and began to write...

'I lived with my parents and nine other siblings in a three bedroomed council house at Beech Crescent, Eckington, a small mining village situated on the Yorkshire and Derbyshire border line...'

By accepting Clive Powell's challenge, I opened up a hornet's nest and wrote everything I could remember that had ever happened to me. It wasn't a conscious decision to write about my abusive childhood, words just seemed to pour out of my mind onto the paper and I couldn't stop writing until I had written the complete story; from as far back as I could recall. After many years I completed my first book, *Little Molly*, then went on to write my second, *Molly II (Am I who I should be?)*. Despite the fact I had never dreamt I would succeed in doing such a thing, it came quite naturally, although I struggled to recall some of the devastating moments that took place, I completed it because I wanted to make a difference in this world and thought, as I still do now, if the likes of John Wass can learn by their mistakes; then my books have been worth writing.

—⁂—

CHAPTER 5

Remembering Eddie

I promised my friend, Eddie, if ever I found justice in this world I would write a third part to my autobiography about the time we spent together before he died and although I made it clear to him I would only tell it as it was, it never seemed to faze him, so although I hesitate, I have decided to write about what we both went through during the last two years of his life.

I cast my mind back to Saturday 11 September 2010. I had just had the biggest row with Eddie over the telephone, it had been over a year since we met up again and in all that time I had not been able to relax. I knew what it is that I feared but I began to rekindle my relationship with him, knowing at the end of it all I would be totally devastated. In the space of a year I had learned he was not the man I met in Old Bolingbroke, but someone who seemed so wrapped up in a family I believed did not care for him the way they should have. In many respects he reminded me of my father when I was a small child when he was so ill he couldn't do the things he used to do for Mother and he was ridiculed for it, he always seemed so pale and wan that I felt sad just looking at him; and I felt that same sadness for Eddie. It had been fifteen years since Eddie and I lived together with our children in Old Bolingbroke, he was a man I had high regard for and I took time to understand him. But since I had learned he was suffering from COPD and hadn't got long to live, the thought of him being estranged from his son, Adam, and leaving his newly born grandson behind; without making amends was almost too much for me to bear. From what I understood, up to March 1999, he had spent fifteen years adapting to the ways of his new partner and her children, only to find for everything he did for them they spent years calling him behind his back and found great satisfaction in discrediting his name hoping he would never find out about it; and yet he still ran to their aid when they beckoned... why? I asked myself. I spent a whole year trying to convince him that he was not, "the ugly" they had nicknamed him and tried my utmost to get him back onto level ground again. But still he occasionally treated me with contempt and I found it impossible to get close to him. I listened to the sad stories he relayed to me over and over again of the lonely times he had experienced and understood his reasons for expecting nothing more from them. His step-daughter, Sam, seemingly had a significant connection with him and despite having nothing much to give, he could not say no to anything she asked of him. Her four-year-old daughter, Codie, seemed to play a significant role in his life and was far more important to him than any other being on this earth. It seemed to me that he used her to fill the space in his life that he felt was lacking and seemed to live for her alone. I wasn't surprised to hear that he took full responsibility for Codie from the day she was born and even when she had reached the age of three she was still the main light in his life.

After being diagnosed with COPD and suffering a terrible bout of pneumonia, he told me he had spent hours each and every day babysitting her and because of that, he formed a bond so tight he was oblivious to everyone around him when he was with her. Her two-year-old brother, Mason, was no more than a shadow of her existence and as far as I could see he was shown very little attention – and occasionally I felt the need to intervene just to remind Eddie that Mason was a baby too and needed an equal amount of love and affection, but it seemed no matter what advice I gave to him it made no difference to the way he was with Codie. The children's birthdays would come and go, and although Mason's birthday was just weeks before Codie's he assured me he could not remember it! After being employed as a bus driver at Colchester Borough Transport for the largest part of his life, he decided to move away from Colchester and work for his niece, but after a year, things became difficult for her and her family, so Eddie was laid off and he found it impossible to get another job. The COPD had taken hold of him, so he resigned himself to being virtually unemployable; then there was simply no turning back. I visited him as often as I could and stayed when I was well enough to, but I was so saddened to watch him deteriorate. The long bouts of coughing and breathlessness were alarming and at times I feared he would die in my arms; but I always remained calm during those moments and did all I could to ease his breathing difficulties. When he first left his niece's home to look for a place of his own, he managed to secure a tenancy with a local landlord in Dover, although it was the top floor of a two-storey building it was fairly close to the town centre and put a roof above his head; at that time that's really all that mattered. My first visit to his bedsit was a bit of a shock, I counted the steps as he led me to a tiny room at the top of the house, forty-four all told; and no lift. I was heartbroken to see where he had ended up but as usual I tried to put a positive outlook on it. I looked through the only window in the room and tried to see through the large mounds of black bags of refuse and rubbish scattered all over the yard and said, "Oh, I see there's an Aldi's supermarket just across the road, at least you won't have far to go for groceries, that's handy!" I hoped he could not detect the disappointment in my voice as I remained facing the window while I tried to control the pressure of tears that were forcing their way out from the corner of my eyes; I took a deep breath in and swallowed hard while I tried to maintain composure. As I slowly turned to face Eddie, I noticed him scouting around his bedsit for loose change, hoping to find enough money to buy a loaf of bread and a bottle of milk. I felt so sorry for him, but I didn't want to embarrass him anymore than he felt already so I waited for him to collect as much change as he had, before suggesting we took a look inside Aldi's. "It's years since I've shopped at Aldi's," I said. "How about we do a bit of shopping while we are in there?" I asked.

"Can do," he replied. I knew Aldi's stocked all kinds of things, including some hardware; so it gave me the opportunity to look around his bedsit and make a mental note of the things he most needed; so I could purchase what I could for him. I recalled how we had lived together with our children as a family at Old Bolingbroke and remembered how much my children had loved him, so it just seemed right I should try to make him a little more comfortable towards the end of his life. After the initial shop, it was something we did often, and I bought enough groceries for him to live on until I saw him again; but as his financial situation slowly worsened he complained of destitution and found life very difficult. He experienced a lot of unnecessary hardships, caused through the lack of help and proper support from "Job Seekers", which resulted in regular unpaid benefits that put him into financial difficulty; but needless to say, as soon as Codie's birthday came around, he scraped up enough money to place inside a birthday card that he had carefully chosen for her, forgetting he had not done the same for Mason until I reminded him; then he enclosed a small amount for him too. He wasn't related to the children and although I found it difficult to believe, he expressed a slight dislike for their mother Sam; despite their regular phone calls and texts to each other. He told me he had lived with Sam's mother Sandra for almost fifteen years alongside her father and informed me that he actually felt closer to him than he did her. I had never seen a man cry for another man like Eddie cried for him when he spoke about his death and I dare say I will never see the love in another man's eyes like the love I saw in his when he recalled the life he had shared with him. I surmised Eddie saw him as a fatherly figure, as he spoke about him like a son would speak of their father. The loss he felt saddened me, and I couldn't help thinking that God always seems to take the best of us first. The relationships he had maintained with Sandra and her family was clearly none of my business but after listening to their relatives speak about Sandra, her father, and the way things where between them... I couldn't help thinking that somewhere along the line there was something amiss. I had lived with Eddie from 1991 to

1995 in Old Bolingbroke and although it had been fifteen years since we had seen each other, I knew him well enough to detect that his life had not been as simple as he had expected it to be when he first left me in Old Bolingbroke.

December 5 2010. I had returned home, and it had been snowing on and off for almost a week and the view of the garden through my office window looked terribly bleak. The leaves had fallen from the fruit trees and had left the dominant evergreens, which took pride of place around the circumference of the garden as winter slowly set in. As night time fell, I could see the silhouette of identical housing structures leaning against the skyline. The birds desperately searched for a safe place to roost, high above the ground in the bare tree tops; away from the prowling cats that invaded my garden during the dark hours. I peered through the window and caught what seemed to be the last few moments of daylight as my eyes remained fixed on the skyline; until the last of the silhouettes had disappeared. As I gazed into the night sky, I caught a glimpse of my reflection through the pane of glass, and once again I realised how much I had changed, how my hair had grown. I took note of the way it cascaded over my shoulders and I smiled at my reflection as I remembered my younger days, when I was back at the Outrake Children's Home when my hair was cut terribly short; I remember I couldn't wait to grow it! At twelve years old I had never experienced the weight of my own hair upon my shoulders and yet I yearned to feel the pride that I observed in other girls as they elegantly tossed their heads and cast their hair aside, away from their eyes. I had been at the Outrake Children's Home for a little over two years and remembered all but one child had short bobbed hair, which seemed to be the most popular style back then and yet so many of us yearned for the beautiful auburn locks that young Anne Molloy prized herself upon. She was the eldest of the Outrake children at that time and rarely suffered at the hands of the staff. From the very first moment she arrived at the Outrake she was made exempt from having her hair cut and yet her younger siblings were made to endure the same ritual that every other child encountered; they had their hair doused with head lice shampoo and regularly raked through with the metal comb, specially designed to trap any louse that had managed to survive the rigorous head washing regimes. Just like myself and every other child who tried to survive the heavy hand of the Outrake staff, they cried but it was something they got used to. Anne Molloy was the typical, freckle-faced teenager who seemed to fit in pretty well from the moment she arrived at the Outrake and, although she looked undernourished and pale, Matron warmed to her and used her as the prime example of perfection. She wasn't someone I got on too well with, yet I became good friends with her younger sister Jane, who like me had dark hair cut so short it didn't even cover her ears. Our hair was very important to us, something we all took pride in and although we became aware of the rules we had to adhere to, it was our crooked fringes and uneven bob cut that many of us cried about each time it was cut!

I was highly delighted when I left the Outrake Children's Home. I immediately grew my hair, as although it was something other people took for granted, we Outrake children thought we would never live to experience it. I suppose I was lucky really, I originated from a family who had the genes to develop masses of thick, course hair quite quickly; which put me in good stead for growing one of the most beautiful heads of hair anyone had ever seen, and within no time at all. Today, I find myself with a very similar hair style to what I had as a young woman, although I am reaching my fifty-third birthday it seems to suit me, and as my alignments are still in my favour, I feel lucky to have aged so well. Although the road has been very rocky, I am grateful for the life I have lived, although it has been devastating at times I am aware that many people have not had a life half as good. As memories of my youth slowly fade away I find myself wondering what bought Eddie and me back together again, was it the excitement of a new beginning or just an easier life around the corner; I really don't know. We both admit that the feelings we once had for each other never really went away and although we desperately tried to rekindle those happy days, something seemed to stand in our way as we desperately struggled to maintain even a close friendship. So much had happened since we lived together at Old Bolingbroke and because he had adopted so many different traits, I found it difficult to accept that he spoke to me in such a way that at times I didn't recognise him. Maybe, my life had not been as bad as I thought over the fifteen years we had been apart; and perhaps Peter Senior had treated me better than I gave him credit for... It seemed so long since I had spread my wings and communicated with the outside world; I no longer knew what was normal. I sometimes wondered if I expected too much from people, was respect for one another no longer part of the modern world, did I really have no right to demand respect and decency from a man I hadn't lived with since

1995? All of these questions I asked myself, while I was trying to come to terms with so many changes. As my brain became fuddled with the accusations and insults Eddie hurled at me. I was struck dumb as he so often reminded me that I was not always right, and repeatedly asked what caused me to feel, think or behave like I did... Suddenly, I wondered if those eight years of counselling were going to hold me in good stead or would his harrowing persecution become the better of me? I felt he purposely treated me with contempt, solely because he had suffered so much emotional abuse that he blamed all the wrong people for the way he had been treated throughout his life; and held everyone but himself responsible for the terrible life he chose.

Although I found it difficult, I made every effort to please him and tried my utmost to turn our lives around to make things better for him but despite my perseverance; it all seemed in vain. I lacked understanding of his long-term health problems and couldn't accept the inevitable or his willingness just to sit back and accept defeat. My nervous disposition seemed to harass him at times and once again I experienced the effects of the terrible stigma and lack of understanding of mental health issues. Eddie had changed over the years, where he once saw only the good, he had a tendency to expect the worst in all things and yet, to the outside world he created this outrageously amusing and quick-witted character and it seemed only I could see through him; and for that he punished himself. I didn't know this man anymore! I looked and observed as he stroked me affectionately but I sensed a kind of resentment within him and yet I knew only too well he would never divulge to me the reason for it. Liable to sudden change he displayed volatility which he so readily blamed me for.... Sometimes he seemed so transparent, I saw in him more than I wanted to, and yet I held my tongue like I had been used to. It had been well over eighteen months since the day I met him in Peterborough, and since that day I had struggled to maintain the same level of stability that I had before I met him, although my life seemed less interesting before, I was far more settled and did not waste half my time trying to work out a man whose words did not match his actions. Yet again, I felt I had let him down when I realised I had been searching for something that wasn't really there. I frequently asked myself, what is it that I am looking for, happiness? Is there such a thing as, "true happiness"? I studied all those who laughed and had fun around us; and all the time I wondered if they were truly happy. Is it possible that happiness is just a passing phase that we all experience at times but have no way of hanging on too? I wasn't sure. This is a strange old world that we live in, yet we all like to think we have a purpose for being here. I convinced myself a long time ago that my sole purpose for being here was to suffer anything that God could throw at me. While others lived their dreams and built perfect lives around me, I was suffering; just as I suffer now. I cannot recall a single day that has gone by that I haven't felt sad and lonely and when Eddie has gone, I will feel alone again. People will look at me and see me smile, they will not see the hurt I feel inside or the love I craved for, they will see only what I portray, a habit that I have found almost impossible to break is 'putting on a brave front'. I found it almost amusing when Eddie compared my personality with his, he had such power to influence people, the true combination of qualities in his own make-up were seldom recognised for what they really were, and I began to wonder if anyone really knew him. I had such doubts about the way he was handling the inevitable, but I did not allow him to see my grief or the concerns I had for him. I reminded myself what had taken place over the period of eighteen months we had spent together; we had argued so much that I questioned whether it was worth all the pain and anguish it caused to cling on to someone who I knew had so little time left.

Before Eddie and I met in Peterborough I was doing really well, I had been seeing my counsellor, Clive Powell, for many years and had managed to write my first book, *Little Molly* and prepare notes for *Molly II* . Since then I have managed to publish them and have written and published a small number of children's books called *Meet the Bubblechomps,* for which Eddie prepared the image formation… But I noticed during the time it took to do all of that his attitude towards me changed. I felt in many respects we clashed, when I tried to offer my opinion or converse with him, especially regarding something he knew very little about, it erupted into a full-blown argument and neither one of us was willing to back down and we usually ended up in tears; apologising for something we both considered was not our fault. As time moved on we recognise we had many differences and tried to overlook the things we didn't like about each other and continued working on the *Bubblechomp* books, hoping to complete a whole series of them before the inevitable happened. I felt we both lacked the sympathy to understand how each of us felt when we were at our lowest, and I constantly told him that he could not treat me like one of Sandra's family, and regularly informed him that I would not allow him to put me into the same category as her. Just like me, Eddie hated giving up a fight and prized himself as the more dominant one; being the youngest member of a family of four Derbyshire boys I could understand why he wanted to be, 'Top Dog' so to speak but as the saying goes, 'Derbyshire born, Derbyshire bred, strong in the arm, weak in the head'. Being born into a large Derbyshire family myself I understand that saying only too well, but throughout the years I had learned not to give up too easily and always tried to give as much as I was willing to take. Like many men, Eddie had chosen to live his life around people who were far weaker than himself, thus enabling him to be the dominant male amongst many. So, when he met me, I think he found it difficult to give up that role to one, whom he considered to be of the 'Weaker Sex'. I felt it was that, which created many problems between us. Although I did not consider myself to be particularly strong – in the sense that I could argue for all I was worth at a rate Eddie and I did without feeling emotional – but as a 'Derbyshire Lass' and a survivor of devastating abuse I must admit I did try and hold my own, as I was reluctant to admit that at times I could be an easy push-over. Although I felt so much love for him, each time we argued I lost a certain amount of faith in him and resigned myself to the fact that the short time we had left to spend together before he died would never be what I expected it to be when we first met.

Each time I returned home from his flat in Dover and spoke to him over the telephone I felt a strange sense of uncertainty in his voice, and occasionally I asked him if he wanted to part company; but he was adamant it

wasn't what he wanted and continued his plight of marriage. As much as I would have liked to have married
him, I wasn't sure it was for the right reasons and so I
delayed my answer hoping he would understand; but in
retrospect I really don't think he did! Eddie and I had
been through so much together that my trust in him was
not what it should have been and despite his continual
pleas to marry me, I just couldn't get the past out of my
head, years previously he had broken my heart. When
he left me and my children in Old Bolingbroke I hadn't
realised that the woman he had introduced me to prior
to that was actually his best friend's sister Sandra,
I couldn't forget that! Despite everything I wanted to be
with him till the end; for no other reason other than I
loved him!' Despite the difficult times we experienced,
he unremittingly accused me of being unbalanced and
regarded me to be the kind of person he could not relate
too; so, I wondered about his reasons for wanting to
marry me? I must admit I began to feel quite inadequate
when I was around him and regularly asked myself why
he had pursued me if he was going to patronize me. He
so often spoke of my distrust in him and the effect it had
upon him, but I learned he had a double standard set of
principles which allowed him greater freedom than I,
within our relationship, and so I wondered if his intentions were truly honourable. When we lived with our
children as a family at Old Bolingbroke I trusted him
with my life, and yet while I tried to reinstate that
feeling of trust, I was unable to relax enough to fully
open my heart and mind to him the way I did back
then! I surmised it would take a lot longer than the two
years we had left to build the same level of trust in each
other as we had back then. I did not pretend to have all

the answers like he blatantly accused me of and I didn't have a magic wand to give him back his health; or make everything right for him. All I had was myself and just like every other human being I followed my instincts, admittedly at times I followed my heart and made a lot of mistakes in doing so but I kept on trying, hoping that one day I would get it right. I often wonder whether I should have saved myself the heartache and disappeared from his life completely but then I remember thinking about our past and all the promises we made to each other. I recall the times when my children were put at ease by him; when they were ill and feeling at their worst. Times too numerous to mention when my daughter Cheniel returned home to us during her access visits, in pain and suffering terrible bouts of what had been termed as 'reoccurring fungal infections' on her feet. Eddie bathed and treated her feet with Mycell athletes' foot cream and nursed her until she had recovered; knowing that the pain she suffered was excruciating. I recalled some of the happiest moments we had together; the trips to Snipe Dales Country Park where we ran and laughed as each of our children played and tumbled over each other as they role-poled down the hills. I recalled our children's contagious laughter echoing throughout the Dales and the joy I felt when I saw how their little faces glowed with excitement as each one of them in turn reached the bottom of the hill, steadied themselves and raced back up again, ready to begin again; all this and more I remembered.

My mind was in turmoil, understanding very little about the lung disease COPD I took on board everything Eddie told me about it and how it affected him. I tried to understand his need to visit the respiratory nurse, Lea, at the Dover health clinic, as often as every other week and yet I found it impossible to understand why they had reasons to call each other as often as twice a week just to confirm those appointments. I panicked a little, thinking the inevitable was closer than I thought and wondered if Eddie was trying to protect me in some way. After numerous appointments with Lea, Eddie allowed me to accompany him to a couple of his appointments, solely to stop me from worrying about things and put my mind at ease but it wasn't as simple as that. I found the more I knew about his condition, the more fearful I became of losing the one person I thought would live for ever. During the appointments I attended I observed that Lea was a clean, rather well-spoken young man, very casually dressed but very polite and understanding, he possessed a lot of knowledge about COPD and captured both Eddie's and my attention when he pulled out large charts of diagrams, illustrating the different stages of the disease and the terrible effects smoking had on the lungs. It was something neither of us had ever thought about when we were in our thirties; when I chose to give up smoking and he chose to carry on. Although we were hoping for a miracle; I think at that stage we both knew he would not survive beyond the six-year life span he was originally given by his GP. Although life proved very difficult, the installation of Eddie's landline seemed to make things a lot easier for him and it took me no time at all to work out that each time he received a call he became very anxious; expecting results from blood tests caused such anxiety and I often found myself vacating the room to give him privacy. I recall one particular time when he first had the phone fitted into his flat, he told me Lea was on the phone and within seconds the atmosphere could have been cut with a knife, so I vacated the room to allow him to speak freely. It became obvious to me at that time that something was wrong, something he didn't want me to know about, I got upset and within ten minutes their conversation had come to an and he was on his way down to the clinic to collect a different type of medication; that's when I knew his health had got worse. The longer I knew him the worse things became and although I did all I could to clear it from my mind, I knew Eddie only had a short time to live – but I didn't want to believe that!

It had been over six years since I took my first steps from my home in Market Deeping to make the short bus journey to Peterborough where I met him. Not a difficult task you might think but at that stage of my life it felt almost impossible; after ten years of isolation It was like coming face-to-face with the devil. I was nervous, and my hands were hot and sweaty, I trembled in my boots as I slowly pulled open the front door, peering and checking that the coast was clear, fearful of people who I had lived around for almost thirteen years. All kinds of terrifying thoughts flashed through my mind as I nervously walked away from the security of my home... What if I go into a panic and freeze with fear, who will help me then? I asked myself. What if I have another seizure, fall and crack my head on the ground? The possibility of falling into the middle of the road terrified me and I asked myself, what if I got hit by a car or I suffer another bout of anxiety and go into hysterics? As my stressful heart beat harder and louder than ever before, flashbacks of all the devastating things that had happened to me throughout my life bombarded my mind as I broke into a cold sweat and tried to make sense of all that was happening to me. Then my thoughts turned to the weather, what if the sky turns black and fierce and it pours down with rain and the wind picks up and brings storms; even as a child I was terrified of lighting and the crack of thunder. But then I stopped for a moment and mumbled to myself, "Don't be silly, catch your breath and take your time." I tried hard to follow my instincts and allow my inner strength to overpower my greatest fears as I tried to calm myself. My heart slowed and seemed to regain normal activity as I gradually move forward; determined to get to my daughter's house before I panicked again. I told myself, if I could just make it there I'd be okay. I still had three quarters of the way to go and regularly checked behind me, calculating the distance between me and my home as I shuffled forward. I became aware of the equal distance between my home and my daughter's, and my fear suddenly rose again, and I began to panic as my breathing became more erratic, I quickened my steps to seek the safety of her home and she greeted me in astonishment. I felt embarrassed, as my youngest daughter had suddenly become my crutch. I wanted to ask her to accompany me to Peterborough, but I knew that wouldn't be right! I wanted to lean on her, so I could fight the phobias that had crippled me for most of my life, and in return I hoped to give her back some resemblance of the mother I used to be; that above everything was what I wanted most. Feeling somewhat shaken and a little foolish, I made the decision to finish what I started out to do, to catch the bus into Peterborough city centre where I had arranged to meet Eddie's family when they set me the challenge.

My daughter offered a simple alternative. "Mum, why don't you wait here and let Mark take you into Peterborough in our car?" she asked.

It would have been much easier had I said yes but I quickly refused so I didn't weaken and take the easy option. "If I don't do this today I will never recover from this awful phobia," I told her.

"Okay but let me come to the bus stop with you," she said.

Although it was only at the top of the road, I agreed, simply because I knew only too well that if I hadn't allowed her to accompany me I would never have made the journey at all that day. A beautiful Sunday morning, and after finally making it up to the bus stop and boarding the bus I nervously sat glaring through the window at her as she waved goodbye; but I could see that she was nervous for me. The driver, perhaps in his early twenties, glanced at me through his front mirror before pulling the bus away from the stop. I felt a little embarrassed as I was so sure he could see how nervous I was, but as he gradually built up speed I tried to hide my fear as the familiar sight of Market Deeping slowly disappeared into the background. The driver followed the signs to Peterborough and I must admit it was the strangest feeling being driven further and further away from home. The bus seemed to take forever before it arrived at the bus station; it was somewhere I wasn't familiar with and crowds of people were stood around the bus shelters waiting for buses to arrive. I was scared and didn't really know where to go, for many years I had been transported to and from hospitals and doctor's surgeries and had forgotten how to do anything for myself and was almost reduced to tears as panic struck, but suddenly amongst the heavy crowds I saw a familiar smiling face that seemed to lift my spirits and helped me to forget the fears I had been burdened with for so many years. Out of the crowds stepped my young friend, Julie, who greeted me with a smiling face and laughter, there was so much excitement, she flung her arms around me with as much warmth as she had when she was a child all those years before; I was amazed that even after fifteen long years she instantly recognised me. She was at the tender age of eighteen when I last saw her; but she had matured into a very attractive, middle-aged mother of two and was just as bubbly and pleasant as she had always been. Her husband Steve had not really changed much since I last saw him, apart from gaining a little weight, he was very much the same man as I remembered. However, their son Danny was a baby in arms when I last saw him, but at the age of fourteen he had grown into a tall, slim, well-mannered boy and his younger sister, Kirston, the youngest family member at the age of nine was a chip off the old block, so to speak. She glared at me with what I would like to think of as admiration, as lots of questions rolled from her tongue and made it very obvious that she was pleased to meet me, and she grasped my hand like she had known me all her life. At that moment in time I thought very little about my state of mind as they made me feel so relaxed. It was difficult to believe that just a few months before I could barely find the strength to leave my home and yet, there I was enjoying time out with friends who I hadn't seen in fifteen years.

As we all began to shuffle our way through the crowds towards the shopping precinct, it was decided a place for coffee would be our first port of call so we could catch up and reminisce about past times, but as I turned towards the escalators that would transport us to the shopping level of the precinct, I caught a glimpse of yet another familiar face. I was stunned and really couldn't believe my eyes, a very warm tender, "Hello, Eddie," left my lips before I even had time to think about the last time I had seen him or the circumstances we had been faced with when we separated fifteen years before. He smiled but hesitated when I asked him if he had been doing okay. His slow responses led me to think that something wasn't quite right but I was sure he would fill me in over coffee. I was overwhelmed to see him because Julie hadn't mentioned bringing him along, he was her favourite uncle so I assumed he had tagged along for the ride and so I greeted him and just went with the flow. I could tell by the warm glow of his smile that he was pleased to see me and of course the feeling was mutual; it seemed we had never lost that spark! As I slowly followed Julie and her family up the well-used escalator to the crowded shopping precinct, I hovered for a few seconds as I reached the top and tried to catch my breath, I wasn't sure where we were heading and at that moment in time I wasn't unduly worried, it seemed just for that moment, after years of being apart, us old friends had come together and we were laughing and joking so much that nothing else seemed to matter; just happy to be together once again! We followed each other through the precinct like a flock of sheep and the aura of excitement we gave off as we laughed at each other's little jokes, while we dodged in and out of the crowds, seemed noticeable to everyone who just smiled to acknowledge awareness as we hurried along, being careful not to lose sight of each other. We ventured in and around the busy town, popping in and out of shops that none of us were familiar with, it seemed that fate had bought us all back together; but all the time I wondered why? We finally arrived at a restaurant just outside the precinct and decided to have coffee there, but after an hour or so Julie and her husband decided to take Danny and Kirston back into the town centre for a little browse, which left Eddie and myself sipping the remainder of our cold coffee before ordering another.

Amongst a very mixed emotional conversation, Eddie broke his devastating news. "I have been diagnosed with COPD, the abbreviation for Chronic Obstructive Pulmonary Disease." And as he paused to catch his breath for a moment I waited for him to finish his sentence. "And, Marie, I only have a couple of years to live!" I was waiting for a follow up sentence like, *unless I stop smoking or the surgeons can operate* but there wasn't a follow up sentence. After a very long silence I leaned across the table where we sat and took hold of his hand, I just didn't know what to say. In the past I had helped so many people to overcome hardships and difficulties that occurred during their lives and had always manage to successfully put their lives back on track; but when I was suddenly faced with something like that, I knew I could not put it right, no matter how much I tried. I knew very little about COPD so we spent a good hour or so discussing it but, it was no good, Eddie was dying and there wasn't a thing anyone could do about it; yet he looked so healthy. I was so pleased to see him; just for that day I tried to block it from my thoughts. He had been my lover and a good substitute father to my children for almost four years, during the time we lived in Old Bolingbroke; but he was slowly and painfully dying. Even at that point I could not imagine life on this earth without him, although we had been apart for many years we bore no malice for the heartache each of us had caused the other and just naturally came together as if that was the way it was meant to be. We spoke about our children who had grown into young men and women and compared notes regarding each of them, life had not turned out for either of us the way we once anticipated but it seemed neither of us was complaining. We were really happy that day, it was like we had been thrown together just to pass the time of day and talk about old times. We parted later after spending hours reminiscing, but I must admit, although I listened to everything he spoke about I really didn't comprehend the seriousness of COPD; or what little time he had left to live. I always said that I believed in fate, but having lost Eddie to death itself I sometimes lose heart and wonder if it is worth believing in anything at all. Eddie died on 17 July 2012, five days after my birthday. He promised me he wouldn't die on my birthday; and somehow, I just knew he wouldn't. We spoke about death well before he died, and he told me that he believed in angels and occasionally when I was feeling bitter about losing the people I loved, I scoffed and told him I wasn't sure if I believed in God anymore. But he regularly told me, "If you don't believe in Jesus you won't go to heaven!" He told me he would be waiting in heaven for me, so I had to believe! After everything that has happened to me during my life, I find it very difficult to believe in anything anymore but I'm really hoping with all my heart that there is a heaven out there somewhere and there are angels taking care of him, I loved him and the thing is, he always said he knew that I did; but it was just a shame I did not have the wisdom to realise it before he died. Eddie's memory will live on in, *The Bubblechomps* children's books that we worked so hard to complete, luckily, we managed to publish just the one before he died but I have another three stored on my computer, ready to be sent up for publication. We worked hard on the *Bubblechomp* series of books and although we didn't always meet eye to eye, we managed to put our differences aside while we worked day and night to complete them, all of which I will one day send up to our publishers to be published, the way he wanted me to; a legacy for our children.

—᎔᎔—

CHAPTER 6

Meeting Sally Welham

September 17 2010. It was a Friday and I had received a notelet through the post. As I opened the envelope and looked inside, I noticed the handwriting on the card was somewhat untidy and difficult to read but as I struggled through it I remembered the day I first met Sally Welham; a local psychologist from the Stamford Resource Centre. She arrived at my home only fifteen minutes after I had returned home under the supervision of Peter Senior; from an emergency visit to my doctor's surgery in Market Deeping. My head was all over the place and I had reached the point where I couldn't control my own life and had finally gone over the top. I had already suffered a breakdown in my early thirties but at the age of forty-two the chances of me recovering from a second one without being committed to hospital were pretty slim. The sound of Sally Welham's quietly spoken voice was the first thing I noticed about her as she entered my home via the front door. I had no idea what was happening to me and in a strange kind of sense I didn't really care. My mind was fixed on one thing and one thing only... giving up! It seemed like I had spent hours sat in front of Dr Wilson that morning, trying to explain to him how I felt and what I thought had caused me to tipple over the edge; I spoke incoherently and had no idea what had happened to me. I was unable to describe the horrific scenes that repeatedly flashed through my mind and I couldn't explain what was worrying me. Each time Dr Wilson spoke to me, his voice echoed inside my head with such an exaggerated sound I couldn't bear to listen to it and I panicked as his voice seemingly beat like a drum inside my head. I found it impossible to recall all that had happened that morning and couldn't even remember leaving the house. I wanted to speak to him and explain what I was doing there but I couldn't form the words; and when he sympathised with me all I could do was cry. Every muscle in my body hurt, my jaws were full of pain and remained rigid with my teeth clasped together. I could not describe how much pain I was in, or the fact that my head felt like it was going to explode, but with Peter Seniors' help I managed to sit through a very small part of a routine oral examination; but failed to make sense of anything that was said.

When I arrived home, I shuffled across to the the large comfy chair in the far side of the living room, just to burrow myself into it; It was the only place I felt safe. It took only minutes for the doorbell to ring after I had sat down, and a team of professional psychologists arrived at my front door. Suddenly I heard a voice, "Hello, Rosemarie! My name is Sally Welham, Doctor Wilson asked me to come and see you," she quietly informed me. "Can you hear me, Rosemarie?" she asked.

I wanted to listen but raised my arms in order to place my hands flat against my ears as each and every word that left her mouth seemingly beat like a drum against my head. Convinced she wouldn't have the expertise to help me, I whispered beneath my breath, "Please don't hurt me, I can't bear it!" I had no idea why I was saying things like that but as she continued to speak, I felt unbearable pain and confusion as she desperately tried to converse with me.

"Can you hear me, Rosemarie?... Rosemarie, can you hear me? I need to know that you understand me and can hear what I am saying."

I tried to raise my head to focus on her face, but I was in such turmoil, the room seemingly swayed from side to side, her image was distorted and I nervously trembled as I sat gripping the sides of the chair; too frightened to let go for fear I fell over. I wondered why she continued to bother me and mumbled to myself, "Go away, please go away." I was hoping, by some unnatural means, I would miraculously recover from whatever it was that was wrong with me, so I could converse with her; but it just didn't happen. It was one of the most difficult days of my life; when I really thought I was going to die. I willed it to happen to make things easier on myself as the pain and suffering was all too much and at that particular time I couldn't think of anything I wanted to live for. The terrible sensations, I was burdened with crawled around my skin like insects gnawing at my flesh and I could feel the heat around my face as I rubbed frantically at my scalp; desperately trying to rid myself of the terrible anguish it caused. Distracted with grief, I searched the house for something to cover my head, hoping to restrict the sensations that almost drove me mad. There was no thought before action and no fear of dying. I struggled to fasten a blue cotton scarf around my head, so I could sleep, and prayed I would never wake up again. But like a hysterical child I rose from the chair and wandered aimlessly across the room searching for something, but not knowing what I was searching for! I listened carefully to a conversation I had with my younger self and cried when I realised how disappointed she was in me. The pretty little girl with the short, bobbed hair stood glaring at me, in a vision so real that I was certain I could have touched her, reluctant to try I backed away from her; fearful of all the knowledge she held of my past. I focussed on her tiny hands as she grasped a small corner of the filthy old blanket she dragged across the floor; 'she blames herself!' I thought. Those words rang repeatedly through my mind as I remembered the terrible abuse I had suffered and knew only too well that I blamed myself. I constantly asked myself... 'Where were you when I needed you?' I seemingly stood in front of the image of my younger self wishing that things had been different and persecuting myself for not being stronger. Disappearing as quickly as she came, she left me standing there all alone. I tugged at the blue scarf I had fastened around my head and pulled it exceptionally tight hoping that, the memory of little Molly would disappear. 'She had no right invading my thoughts,' I told myself. I had long since forgotten about her, but I was certain she had been there! All of a sudden, I realised that Sally Welham had left my home. Having no sense of time I wondered what day it was and how long I'd been there, somehow, I managed to alert Peter Senior and felt comforted by his presence as I swayed from side to side, closed my eyes and drifted back to sleep. Every time I woke up it seemed I had dreamt about my entire life in just a few seconds and couldn't clear the haunting memories of little Molly and the child abuse from my head.

For years I had been blaming myself for the unsettled life I afforded my children. Following the breakup of mine and Nigel Hadfield's relationship, I was taunted with guilt, plagued with sad memories that reminded me of the heartache and sorrow my children had suffered, but I asked myself: who was to blame really? During my final attempt to bring my daughter, Cheniel, home the judge exonerated me and I recall the shock on Nigel Hadfield's face as he was pulled over the coals for his continual lying inside the court room. I had spent seven long years trying to prove I was a fit mother but I was so naïve and ill with worry that when his solicitor threatened to seek unwarranted justice and have me imprisoned if I persisted in telling the judge that Nigel wasn't Cheniel's biological father, I panicked and abstained from repeating the things I had previously told him – solely because I did not fully understand the concept of the law, and was petrified at the thought of going to prison.

It was at that stage of my life I began to wonder what was really going on; the whole procedure was just like a game of charades and in my opinion had nothing much to do with Cheniel or her siblings' welfare. Cheniel was a statistic, a plain and simple statistic, who, in my opinion, was used as a pawn to aid an acrimonious man to seek revenge. I recall I was astounded with some of the things that were allowed to go on behind closed doors. David Barlow, who was the court welfare officer assigned to the case, was asked to make an unbiased report regarding Cheniel and her welfare, but it took me only an hour during the long appointment with him to realise he had already been influenced by Nigel Hadfield's affidavit and was convinced I was an incompetent mother; who was incapable of piecing a simple sentence together. At first,

I thought he was just being prejudiced because I was a young woman fighting for my rights but then I realised it was more than that. During subsequent appointments he and Nigel Hadfield seemed to collaborate and ran through my family history condemning me for all the abuse I had suffered. They included the sexual abuse I had suffered as a young child, which they eventually used in the court room, hoping it would be one more thing they could hold against me. But after considering the facts, the judge had the whole thing struck from the records; informing everyone in the court room that it should never have been included in the custody case battle at all. But of course, it was already too late, a synopsis of the facts was cunningly implanted into the minds of everyone who sat inside that court room; and in my opinion influenced the judge's initial decision to leave my daughter with Nigel Hadfield. It seemed from that moment on, no matter what I said, my word seemed unworthy and my children suffered unnecessarily for something that wasn't their fault. Cheniel was aged four and a half years old when Nigel Hadfield received custody of her, and my eldest son, Ian, was aged nine. Fortunately, the twins were just over a year old and knew very little of what went on around them, however during the years that followed, just like me, they all suffered greatly from the consequences of it all. It was nothing for me and my children to spend all night crying for each other, wishing the days away hoping that the weekends would come around faster so that we could go and collect Cheniel from Nigel Hadfield's place. I remembered our Sundays before he had received full custody of her; it was my favourite day of the week, my four children enjoyed playing games together and I cooked a large

Sunday roast with plenty of mash and fresh vegetables, a tradition set by our elders. But when the courts gave Nigel Hadfield custody of Cheniel, Sundays just didn't seem the same – and travelling one hundred and twenty miles to return her to his home in Staveley took its toll, and Sundays became the worst day of the week. It took hours for me and my children to travel to Staveley, all of us seemed on edge and I constantly checked my watch to ensure I didn't run late as I absolutely dreaded the consequences of arriving at his place after the court's specified time; for fear of being held in contempt and being sent to prison.

The memories of such heartbreak are always there at the back of my mind and occasionally plague me in my sleep! Throughout the years of trying to raise my children I spent much of my time suffering ill health and struggling to do a decent job of caring for them. Unfortunately, I didn't get the support I needed and because of that things didn't turn out the way they should have done! When Cheniel still lived with us as a family, travelling in the car was considered a treat but she had been dragged from pillar to post so much that by the time she was aged five she hated it, and closed her eyes for the largest part of the journey; all the way back to Nigel Hadfield's. It took me a long time to realise that she wasn't always asleep like I originally thought but kept them tightly closed so she didn't have to explain to her siblings why she was crying... I wondered if the courts would have favoured that! I could not erase the past or control the dreams that taunted my children; but day by day I tried my utmost to make amends for all the heartache they had suffered. I thought long and hard about my children's lives. I had heard so much about human rights but never really understood who those rights were put into place for. If the courts did not get it quite right, where did families who were burdened with so much grief, anxiety and unnecessary pain go to seek justice? I have never been sure, as Cheniel or her siblings were never given choices; no choices and no justice!

After years of applying to the courts to have Cheniel returned to me, David Barlow decided to interview Cheniel, so he could submit a report to the courts. She was around seven years old when he asked her to give him some indication of what she really wanted; did she want to live with me (her mum) and her siblings in the small country village in the heart of Lincolnshire, where we lived as a family, enjoyed picnics, family bike rides and visits to the seaside that was only nine miles away? Or did she want to live with Nigel Hadfield, a single man who lived in a two bedroomed high rise flat; who at that time had no parenting skills whatsoever, socialised in his local public houses and often went home drunk? David Barlow led Cheniel to believe the choice was solely hers; then subtly let her down when she chose to live with me. I could not believe the tactics of the court welfare officer. I suspected much before then, that he was biased and didn't really want to make a report in my favour, but when Cheniel asked me why he wouldn't let her come home after promising her, I realised that the report he had submitted to the courts did not correspond with the choice Cheniel had made!

I understood only too well that children sometimes said things they thought parents wanted to hear, and for years I wondered if Cheniel had chosen to live with Nigel Hadfield. But from the very moment her interview with David Barlow was over she always maintained that she had made it perfectly clear, to both him and his female colleague, that all she wanted to do was live with me and her three siblings. When the court enrolled David Barlow as the court welfare officer he was asked to be definitively clear about his findings and his recommendations, which they said had to be in Cheniel's best interest. But to my knowledge there was no consideration given to her wishes or her feelings, no consideration made for her three siblings; and no regard to the unnecessary breakup of my young family. Mine and Nigel Hadfield's relationship seemed to get worse once David Barlow was enrolled as the court welfare officer. After what I now consider to have been intimidation through tyranny, I became too nervous to attend the recommended appointments with David Barlow and Nigel Hadfield, as previous meetings had become rather heated where both men seemed to side with each other and I ended up in tears and couldn't sit through the meeting, which made it virtually impossible for him to submit the appropriate reports to the courts. So, once again, I was categorised as being uncooperative and was made to feel that it was entirely my fault. Like so many other things, it was held against me and in my opinion affected the judge's decision not to allow my daughter home. It seemed by the time the hearing was over I wasn't just branded an unfit mother but made to feel like a criminal as well.

I recall the morning I was almost arrested and shipped off to Newhall ladies prison, the penalty for failing to attend a court hearing; which resulted in a judge charging me with contempt of court. Nigel Hadfield was considerably thoughtful that weekend, despite the Judges orders he allowed me to keep Cheniel from Friday until Tuesday. He had previously explained to me that he had an appointment on the Monday, so if I wanted to keep her until the Tuesday he'd be able to keep the appointment. Of course, I accepted without hesitation, she was my daughter and I loved her, I wanted to spend every minute of every day with her, but he had lied to me once again and had concocted some story in a bid to teach me a lesson; which he later admitted to his solicitor and the arresting officer who was present at the time. After keeping his previously planned appointment with David Barlow on the Monday morning he proceeded to file court proceedings against me. He told the judge that I had not returned Cheniel on the Sunday evening as ordered by the courts and feared I may keep her; just one more lie that he told on oath! Unfortunately, I could not prove otherwise and just to top it all, I hadn't received the letter ordering me to attend court that morning, so was not only charged with failing to attend court but contempt of court as well. It was only due to the fact that the summons had arrived later than expected, by second class post, while the arresting officer was reading out the judge's order to commit me to prison, that I managed to get the order revoked. Had it not been for that I would have been handcuffed and arrested in front of my four children; and sentenced to prison for nothing more than doing what I thought was right! It seemed that Nigel Hadfield had not expected the judge to make an order to commit me to prison but simply pull me over the coals, so to speak. The lies he told on oath stood him in good stead and were used against me, and for that, me and my children suffered! It was all of this and more that contributed towards the terrible breakdowns and mental health problems I have suffered throughout the years.

—◊—

CHAPTER 7

My Visit to New Zealand

(Reminiscing)

New Zealand is the country my daughter, Cheniel, calls her home and for the first time in her life she is totally relaxed and at peace with herself. I feel she is happy and content; although at times I detect her continuing need to spread her wings and fly. At the age of twenty-seven she finds her biological clock ticking away at a speed she had never anticipated, with so much to see and so much to learn she swiftly moves from one place to another, absorbing as much knowledge of the world as she possibly can. At last I have no fear of losing her and find that the twenty-four-hour flight from England to New Zealand to visit her no longer seems a decade away. Happy with her decision to marry her Kiwi partner, Mike, a native to New Zealand, I no longer worry about her welfare or the effect her traumatic childhood had upon her; instead I feel confident that he and his family will look after her and keep her safe. Having obtained her citizenship, Cheniel worked hard to obtain a place at university to continue her studies, happy in the thought that she would pass her exams and gain her Honours. It was her birthday yesterday! I was so pleased to be able to share it with her. After visiting Te Puna Quarry Park with her and her pet dog Mac, a beautiful well-trained Labrador, I enjoyed watching Cheniel and Mike play touch rugby for Zesprie, the company which Mike worked for; although I didn't quite grasp the rules of the game I really enjoyed the thrill of it all. Their lives are so full and exciting, and I found at the tender age of fifty-three I tired more easily and, as much as I tried, I could not keep up with their active lifestyle. Spending time with Cheniel was like stealing a cherry off a cake; I couldn't think of anything I would have liked to have done more than that.

24 February 2011. I was a long way from home and feeling a little homesick, Eddie wasn't helping, soon after we had arrived in New Zealand he seemed to alienate me and became very hostile when Cheniel and Mike weren't around. Although he tried hard not to let it interfere with them, his feelings where made quite clear when we spent time alone. He gave me the impression he would have rather have been anywhere but there and only portrayed happiness when they were around. We argued at the drop of a hat and spent a considerable amount of time sat in the garden in silence ignoring each other; just as we did back home. He often referred to me as being stupid and I was beginning to wonder if he was right, as despite my better judgement I allowed him to manipulate me into doing only what he expected of me and said only what I felt he wanted me to say; a habit I have never been able to break since childhood. He aggressively suggested that I should stop "thinking"; after almost two years of suggestive remarks like that I felt myself slowly retreating to a state of withdrawal. He used to be so kind to me, but since he found out his COPD had gotten much worse he

had become a hot-headed creature who no longer displayed patience; and I was too old to retreat into my shell just to allow him verbal control. I tried to understand more about his declining health condition and asked what I could do to comfort him, but I failed to realise how serious it all was. At that moment in time I could not accept what little time he had left; and was angry of the fact that he did not appear to want to fight it! I angrily asked him, "Do you want to die?" At that point we would both end up in tears knowing he really didn't have a choice in the matter; he was dying and there was nothing either of us could do about it. I was absolutely devastated but had no idea how to handle it. I agreed to visit New Zealand with him, as he hadn't seen Cheniel since she was a little girl and desperately wanted to see her one more time. Although I feared the long flight and knew only too well he may have fallen ill during the trip, I figured if Eddie was willing then so was I. It was Cheniels birthday party; a modest gathering of family and friends that disguised the terrible atmosphere between Eddie and me as we tried to mingle with the friendly locals. I endeavoured to see the evening through without the interruption of anxiety or tears... something I suffered from when I found myself in the middle of a situation I didn't feel comfortable in. Mike was unwell that day, but still he focussed upon everything that had to be done to ensure Cheniel's birthday was a relatively happy one. I recognised many good qualities in him and feel I owe him a very big thank you for taking such good care of her. Together, they are a match made in heaven; I am sure of that!

Silence is a very strange thing. Having left the rest of my family back in England, I sat in Cheniel and Mike's dining room listening to the unfamiliar sounds of the native birds of New Zealand, but as beautiful as it was I could not enjoy the full extent of their harmonious chorus without feeling sad and empty. Yet again the interaction with Eddie created sadness within me and while we battled through long silences, we suffered the loneliness that only we had created. Yet again he was cold towards me and I felt like I hated him for it, as my mind searched for reasons to approach him, hoping to make amends; I could not. I forfeited my happiness once again to prove that I was no longer as weak as he so often recalled. As I sat alone I began to question my ability to be a good mother, already I had felt that I had let Cheniel down and didn't match everyone's expectations, I tried to think positively but as much as I tried, I found that my own inferiority created even more uncertainty.

New Zealand was a holiday of a lifetime and yet I felt both Eddie and I had chosen the wrong person to share it with. When I was a young woman my mother often reminded me of the quotation, 'Better the devil you know than the devil you don't!'. I never forgot that quotation, and it often reminded me that the grass was not greener on the other side of the fence like we sometimes thought. I had travelled thousands of miles from England to New Zealand to make a decision I ought to have made before I went. Having spent a lot of my time around Eddie and his family I realised I wasn't the person he wanted to spend the rest of his life with. I was tired of playing games with him and even after two long years of trying to build bridges, I knew he would never be capable of loving me like he once did, so my mind was made up. I had to try and wean myself away from him. I knew I would miss him and certain members of his family, but I knew I wouldn't miss all that terrible uncertainty. So much had happened since we had met up again and although I knew I would probably regret it, I realised his life was far too full and complicated for me to be part of it. Although I experienced my fair share of ups and downs in the fifteen years we had been apart, my life had been nothing like his. In respect of my health, I had climbed the ladder and had no intention of returning to the bottom rung of it. I had moulded myself into a far better person than some of his family gave me credit for, and despite their attempts to demoralise me, I managed to remain level headed and ignored his repeated suggestions to "dress down" in an attempt to slot into his large circle of friends and family; who had labelled me "a snob". Although I found New Zealand to be a magnificent place, I regretted the devastating circumstances surrounding Eddie who, for some reason went out of his way to ruin my first visit. It seemed we had spent most of our time moping around and talking about the people he had left back in Colchester and he only bucked up when Cheniel and Mike were around. I found it really difficult trying to keep the terrible atmosphere away from them, but at one stage even Cheniel noticed something was amiss and asked if Eddie and I had been arguing. I couldn't lie so I tried to explain, leaving as much detail out as I could so not to upset her. I found myself in unusual circumstances, I had never been around anyone who was suffering from a terminal disease and although my heart felt like it was bursting with sadness I really didn't know how to handle it. He regularly told me that he didn't want me to feel sorry for him and I knew he wouldn't have thanked me if I'd have waited on him hand and foot, so

I kept my distance so as not to stifle him; but all the time hoping he would live until he had reached the age of a hundred.

8 March 2011. Cheniel and Mike took their dog Mac for a walk on the beautiful beach of Maunganui that evening, while Eddie and I prepared dinner. When they returned an hour or so later they looked smitten and were really happy. Cheniel was wearing part of a beautiful shell that Mike had found on the beach and it fitted nicely around her wedding finger; she danced around the kitchen supporting her left hand with her right and elegantly placed her fingers out in front of me as she proudly displayed what she thought was the most beautiful work of art she had ever seen, and now meant so much to her. She spieled off what I thought to be the most romantic proposal of marriage I had ever heard. "Mum, we have just got engaged, me, Mac and Mike," she said. "Mike found this shell ring on the beach and got down on bended knee and asked me to marry him," she told me proudly!

"And did you accept?" I asked.

"Of course!" she replied.

And so, he betrothed her with a ring from the ocean... I was so proud of them. Her face gleamed and her eyes sparkled, if he had proposed any other way it would not have been the same... she was happy at last!

9 March 2011. Eddie and I endeavoured to climb, Mount Maunganui, having failed once before I doubted my ability to succeed but I volunteered to try one more time; after I had spent the whole week doing light exercises to strengthen my legs. As I proceeded to climb

the wooden steps at the foot of the mount, I could feel the muscles in my legs tensioning. I began to pant almost immediately as it had been such a long time since I had attempt anything remotely similar but having prepared myself for it I tried hard to see it through as I slowly made my way up the sides of the lushest green slopes. I wondered what it was at the top of the mountain that fascinated so many different cultures, as I wandered past the people who had already achieved the steep climb I kept on moving forward all the time telling myself, 'come on, Marie, you have to do this!' Determined not to disappoint everyone, I gathered my thoughts and promised myself I would make it to the top; if only to proudly boast that I had done it! It was basking hot and the midday sun shone down on the back of my shoulders and I was hot and sweating but at that particular moment I couldn't have cared less. While struggling to keep an even pace I thought about Cheniel who had been in New Zealand for over two years. I missed her so much, that when I was back in England my heart ached to be near her, but finally after all her years of travelling I was just a stone's throw away from her and couldn't think of any other time I had felt happier; in just a few hours I would be spending even more time with her! Her university days were proving to be busy ones, so we had to steal short periods of time when she was free to be together but at least I was in the same country as her; if only for a few more days. I wanted to make her proud... even if the climb killed me! Step by step I struggled to follow others along the gravel-filled pathways, gradually ascending towards the top of the mountain; trying so hard not to be a defeatist, I turned my concentration to the very few flowers that grew in clumps on the mountain side and the beautiful view of the ocean. The muscles in my legs had become tense and hurt but I tried to persevere; as I had done during many times of my life. I struggled with the climb but tried to focus on other things while I was doing it and thought about my life back in England, my children, Ian, Kyle and Allishia came to mind and I thought, how much they would have loved to have been there. I thought about Cheniel and Mike and how spontaneously he had proposed to her while walking on the beach. I couldn't remember what had been said, only what had happened when she had accepted his proposal and I recalled the exquisite detail of the broken shell that she wore on her wedding finger; proudly pronouncing the seal of their engagement. I smiled to myself when I realised how beautiful they are together. I thanked God for granting at least one of her childhood wishes. Throughout the years I had been praying so hard that God would give her a break and she would live the rest of her life happy and content; now I know she will! The path up the mountain got steeper and I began to wonder how much further I had to go before I reached the top. Much younger people were struggling to get past me and for the first time in my life I felt envious of the younger generation but then remembered how fit I was in my day. A succession of triumphant climbers descended the mountain and passed by me; cheerfully informing me on how much further I had to climb before I reached the top. "Around the corner and just a few steps more!" I heard one of them say. I desperately wanted to make a success of it for two reasons, to overcome my fear of heights and to make my daughter proud. Finally, I reached the point where I could view man shuffling around like tiny ants on the ground and I suffered a terrible bout of vertigo and froze with fear; just as I always had when I was a child. At that point my mind went into turmoil and I began to panic, I became agitated and confused and knew the time had come to accept defeat and so I reluctantly turned around and made my way back down the mount. I was so disappointed and felt sick at the thought of letting her down but then I recalled her saying, "Mum if you don't succeed this time you could try again next time." I smiled to myself as I gradually descended the beautiful beast of a mount and knew only too well that for her I would do anything!

—◆—

CHAPTER 8

Trying to Find Inner Peace
(DOVER)

June 20 2011. My life seemed to turn a corner. Since I got back from New Zealand, Eddie and I had gone our separate ways and although we still occasionally spoke on the telephone we made no plans to see each other again. I think I knew him well enough to realise at that point of his life he preferred to be with his family rather than end his days with me. So, when I met Drew I thought it was something we all call 'destiny' and my life would never be the same again. During our first encounter I wasn't sure what to make of him; I had heard lots of stories about him, some good but some un-pleasantries, still, the thing I seemed to focus on was that he gave refuge to the homeless and the vulnerable. I recall when Eddie had no place to call his own and was searching for somewhere to live, the housing department at Dover gave him Drew's telephone number, knowing even if he hadn't got the room he would fit Eddie in somewhere! Drew was so well known in those parts he was able to contact friends and acquaintances to find places for the vulnerable but Eddie was lucky, he got to stay in one of Drew's bedsits; so, he didn't end up on the streets, homeless and destitute. After listening to the way Eddie spoke about his landlord, I thought there must be some good in this man! I really liked the fact that he housed so many vulnerable people but up until meeting him I was given the impression he was some kind of ogre and that many residents hated him. He owned many properties around Dover and surrounding towns and I think it was because of that; he knew many influential people who showed him a lot of respect but there were the occasional few who seemed unhappy with Drew's rules and expectations as a landlord, which didn't help his reputation! I have always believed that there is a certain amount of good in everyone but when I saw some of Drew's tenants I began to wonder, they were total outcasts, abusive and raw, and for a while I felt intimidated by them but after a while I became a little concerned about the men who occupied the majority of the bedsits; although they looked a little worse for wear I was sure they were better than the reputation some people gave them. It took me some time before I realised that some of the men who looked anxious and worn were veterans who had served in the British army, but since coming out and falling on hard times they ended up living in one of Drew's bedsits; sharing a bathroom and kitchen with drug addicts and alcoholics. I must admit I was alarmed by some of the stories the men told, although I had lived in much worse conditions when I was a child, the circumstances of those who had fought for our country just did not seem right... I sat inside Eddie's bedsit many hours listening to the banter of ex-squaddies, and for the first time in my life I realised how much of their life they forfeited to serve our country! To pass the time away while I was staying with Eddie I wrote poetry, about everything that touched his life. I listened to all his stories about life in the army and how much he loved serving his country alongside his older brothers; one, who I believe was ranked as a Major. So, it made me wonder, how on earth did he end up in a poor man's bedsit, struggling for his breath? I dedicate the poem *Ex-Squaddies* to all ex-squaddies, particularly Eddie and his brothers.

—∭—

Ex-Squaddies

I mingled with lots of men...
Young fit soldiers they were back then.
Dressed as civilians to fit the part;
Their banter was heard right from the start.
Self-loading rifles; they recalled the past...
How they fired them with a blast.
Soldiers wounded; some were bound,
Others lay lifeless on the ground.
Morbid sights; their flashbacks recalled...
Some ex-soldiers still live through it all.
Memories... ought to have been buried with the past;
Still live on, remembering the last World War
Where their granddads and their dads;
Made a stand for their young lads.
Families overcome by grief.
Two minutes silence is not enough;
To remember soldiers; who they loved.
They fought with courage and with strength
To bring a world of violence to an end.
Written by Rosemarie Smith

I got to know Drew when he began to confide in me, he told me that he developed properties and enjoyed a rather successful business that afforded him an enjoyable and relaxing lifestyle; living in some of the most outstanding areas of Kent. Despite meeting his parents a couple of times, it was really only when I volunteered to accompany Eddie as an amateur painter to help him work off the debt he owed for the bond for his bedsit that I realised, had it not been for that he could not have afforded the deposit for his bedsit and would have remained homeless. By painting and decorating parts of a property Drew's family had purchased he was able to pay off a bond, that by rights as a man with a terminal disease should not have been paying at all; instead the council should have given him rebate to cover it! Unfortunately, Eddie's homeless circumstances forced him into accepting unsuitable accommodation from Drew and working at a rate that was considered to be less than the minimum wage at approximately £4.75 per hour. It proved to be gruelling work for a dying man; and even after months of hard labour he still hadn't been able to work off the money he owed to Drew. Eddie worked very long hours but didn't think to keep an official record of all the hours he had worked, so never really knew when or if his debt to Drew would ever get paid off. It wasn't until summer 2010 that I eventually realised that Drew did not have full knowledge of Eddie's health conditions, or how many hours he had worked, as Eddie had been given the keys to the property and was painting the outside of the building during the hot summer evenings to take his mind off dying. It seemed that Drew was unaware of all the hours Eddie put in, although Eddie's debt to them had long since been paid. When I found out that Eddie was working for nothing, I advised him to discuss it with the family when Drew returned from his vacation abroad. When Eddie finally got chance to discuss it with them, he was so ill he wasn't really interested in the money, however, Drew paid the amount he thought he owed – but it wasn't the amount it should have been! Eddie was one of the very many vulnerable people who relied on benefits to pay deposits to secure a tenancy and cover rent for a room they might not have otherwise had, but Eddie said they didn't pay his and he was forced to repay a debt that in my eyes the council should have paid alongside his housing benefit. It is only now after Eddie's death, that I cast my mind back and realise what fools we were. Drew, by all accounts, was a very powerful, successful businessman from Dover and although I do not see any wrong in being successful, I do believe it's thanks to our government and certain laws of our country that much of Drew's success came to him via people's downfall and vulnerability.

Having had the privilege of staying at Drew's beautiful cottage for almost a year, I questioned in my own mind as to whether he offered me a, "quiet and ideal place to write," out of the goodness of his heart or to lure me into his clutches. Trusting, sympathetic and over-generous is what people recognise in me and after many years of constantly trying to defend my good nature, I realise it is not actually something I should be ashamed of; despite the fact it has very often led to me being used, abused and taken for granted. When I first accepted Drew's invitation to stay at his cottage I was over burdened with family problems and had recognised a decline in my mental health, so after many lengthy telephone calls and persuasive texts from him, I accepted an offer I thought was too good to refuse. He said, "I have an eighteenth century thatched cottage with a beautiful large garden where you can write in the summer, you can have your own bedroom and I can turn the single guest room into an office for you; for when the weather is unfit." After mulling things over for a couple of weeks, I accepted his very generous offer and looked forward to visiting him at the cottage as he had told me so much about it. Having lived in a council property most of my life, being given an opportunity to stay somewhere like that was something only dreams were made of. The evening I arrived, Drew had driven all the way from Dover to pick me up from my home in Market Deeping, just as we arranged. It was my birthday, and he suggested it would be a good day to meet as we could call at his local pub on the way and open a bottle of wine once we arrived at the cottage. Having corresponded with him for some time I thought it was possible I may have allowed Eddie's experiences to cloud my judgement regarding Drew and really looked forward to spending time with him. After a very long journey we arrived at the cottage early in the evening when it was raining. Drew had parked his truck just in front of the post-office red, Tudor-designed door at the front of the cottage and climbed out of his truck to unleash the heavy tarpaulin from over my suitcases; which had been protecting them from the rain. As I remained seated in the cab, I watched him unleash the cover in the rain, he was built solid and strong and stood over six feet tall and his shoulders were at least three feet across at their widest point; not a man to mess with I thought. I jumped out of the cab and helped to unload my suitcases from his old, battered, pick-up truck, despite its dented sides and morbid greyish colour he seemed genuinely proud of it – more so than his beautiful red, Jaguar sports car that looked like it had been carelessly parked on the gravelled driveway; just right of the cottage. The three-and-a-half-hour journey from my home was not the most comfortable ride I had ever had but I arrived in one piece, which was quite astonishing considering the state of the truck. I was really excited at the thought of having somewhere as beautiful as 'Hop Cottage' to write part of my autobiography. I entered the front door and the first thing I noticed was the unusual odour, a mixture of ageing wooden beams and burning logs that lay smouldering in the bottom of the log fire, not unpleasant but nothing like I had ever experienced before. Drew had gone out of his way to make my stay as comfortable as possible and told me so, he said he had extended his cleaning lady's hours so she could make an exceptional job of cleaning inside the cottage before I got there and employed someone to maintain the garden. He went on to say that the place had been checked over and any repairs that needed doing had been carried out by his closest friend, whom he referred to as 'Deano', who apparently doubled up as his chippy, plumber and electrician! They had a good rapport with each other and as far as I could understand, Deano was good at his job and always on call; of course, this was necessary because of the amount of properties Drew and his family owned. Me and Deano never really hit it off, right from the word go it seemed there was a wedge between us, I wasn't really sure whether it was me or Deano that created the atmosphere when all three of us were together; not until Drew volunteered information that helped me to understand why we never really got on. Drew had never had time for many steady girlfriends or long-standing relationships before he met me, so according to him, Deano may have been a little jealous. My opinion of Deano was very limited, although he was a very attractive, muscular young man who women seemed to drool over I felt he went out of his way to make me feel uncomfortable and his mannerisms did not impress me; so, I spent very little time in his company. I actually got on better with Drew's more influential associates who he solely used to benefit his business; however, they seemed to like me and treated me with the greatest respect.

Hop Cottage was a typically eighteenth century dwelling with lots of character and beautiful features, the type of place one falls in love with, however once I had stepped over the threshold I found it very dull and uninviting, it was morbid-looking and kind of creepy. When I first arrived, and Drew asked me what I thought of the place, my opinion was that the interior did not coincide with the beautiful exterior, garden and grounds that were lavishly adorned with beautiful flowers, trees and shrubs of all species and ample space to house even more. The smell of smouldering wood lingered about the rooms and the huge wooden fire surround showed telltale signs of misuse. Charcoal and ash had been scooped up into an old brass bucket on the right side of the hearth and a considerable number of logs were piled up on the other side of a well-used log burner that took up at least two thirds of the hearth. An abundance of fruit filled an unusually large wooden fruit bowl that had been placed in the centre of an olde-world carved coffee table that was laden with magazines and newspapers of all descriptions – covering its best attributes of two-toned wood grain. The aroma of beeswax furniture polish lingered about the room which really complemented the smell of the hot cinders that lay at the bottom of the fire grate. Orange peel had been thrown into a large wicker basket at the side of the hearth, presumably left for the cleaner to remove, and a large bronze-effect Marilyn Monroe figurine dominated the study, putting the less obvious bric-a-brac into the shadow, yet together they created a warmth to the poorly-lit sitting room that I was led into. A well-used ox-blood-red Chesterfield suite took up a large proportion of the room and a matching leather-topped desk stood in the large bay window that created a source of light in the room. Sunflower yellow walls set the perfect background for the dark wooden beams and the reclaimed, oak floor boards. A framed Constable print was hung above the mantle and an old 40's style lamp hung inside the recess next to it, giving the whole room the perfect resemblance of an eighteenth century cottage. The dark, wooden gate-effect door had been roughly made and opened via a black metal pull-down catch that looked quite unsightly, but Drew said he was very pleased that the shoddy workmanship gave the effect he was hoping for; to replicate its original state. As I walked towards the kitchen I stepped down a few shallow wooden steps that took me level with the beautiful flagstone flooring that complimented the old cottage-style kitchen which had been adorned with dried flowers, wheat and barley which draped naturally over the top of the kitchen units. A large array of flowers stood in the window above the kitchen sink; gracing the whole room with elegance. A large pine table and chairs stood at the back of the room, dressed with an orange and lace table-cloth which was slightly stained on one side; making it obvious to me that someone had eaten a meal at the table and carelessly spilt food. I had spent only minutes inside the cottage before Drew showed me a simply furnished bedroom large enough to fit the beautiful pine bed and matching wardrobe he had purchased specifically for me and said, "You could sleep in there!" It wasn't a very feminine room but the beautifully made drapes hung at the windows complemented the duvet and brightened the room! I recall he left me alone for a couple of hours while he walked across to his local club, giving me time to unpack and try, unsuccessfully, to fit all my clothes into the limited drawer space beneath the wardrobe as he had not purchased coat hangers and I hadn't thought to pack any!

Suddenly, my mind drifts to a rather enjoyable evening we spent together in the newly furbished conservatory that was exquisitely designed and decorated with an array of historic bric-a-brac from bygone days. Three different species of orchids were in full bloom and stood in a wooden trough that complemented them, while a huge, solid, rustic wooden coffee table stood in the middle of the room; giving it an authentic look. A mass of mustard coloured voile was draped from the roof of the conservatory and gave it a romantically warm, Arabian feel. I was enthralled by its splendour and thought it must have taken thousands of pounds, time and effort to achieve such a beautiful effect to a room; he was exceptionally proud of it!

The impression I got of Drew that night was one of despondency, the music he repeatedly played portrayed him to be a sad and lonely person; I felt tearful for him. The romantic love song, *The Blower's Daughter,* sung by Damien Rice seemed to play a significant role in his life, as he played it over and over again and so I learned the song very quickly and the lyrics stuck inside my head. I thought the romantic songs and the atmosphere he had created depicted the way he felt about me, but as time moved on I began to think I meant no more to him than any other person he had dated. It seemed the very few women he had dated hoped one day he would pop the question and ask them to marry him, but not me. I had already been told by several people that he wasn't the marrying kind, that he was someone who stripped a woman of everything they owned then disregarded them, never taking into account their feelings; but of course, I had never been one for listening to gossip. In comparison to many, Drew was huge in both his structure and popularity, despite constantly informing me that he had very few real friends or people he could trust, I found he and his family practically governed the whole population of Dover and apart from his son and the varied drop-outs, it seemed to me he had everyone eating out of his hands. He and his son had not spoken for some time and although I tried to understand Drew's explanation as to why they didn't speak, I couldn't get my head around it. Their disputes had a whole backlog of history, dating back to the early nineties but I tried not to get involved and didn't delve too far into it. My relationship with Drew was one that we put everything we had into, but tried not to depend on one another financially. I didn't have much money, although I do believe he surmised otherwise and began to rely on me to pay for the majority of our food and other things that we required. I now believe he was under the impression I was a very successful author with no financial limitations, so the more I gave the more he expected but I eventually found it impossible to keep up with it. For a man in his position I found it almost impossible to believe he could take advantage of me in that way. My writing was solely therapeutic which gave me a sense of purpose but gradually I felt he was even taking that away from me. Our relationship got to the stage where he knew all my incomings and outgoings, and even an accurate account of the amount of credit that was available on my credit cards. Of course, it took me a while before I realised he was no amateur and according to his own admittance he had treated several woman this way, but always referred to it as doing "his job" – and I was supposed to be grateful! His regular persuasive offer of becoming my manager if I was to do as he said and enter the world of, "upper class escorts" fell on deaf ears, so to speak and I ignored his proposals – although at times he became frustrated at the thought of me ignoring him. "I will show you the routine and you will make me a very rich man!" he informed me. By that time, he was well aware that I was on the borderline of poverty so took advantage of my circumstances and desperately tried to pressurise me into becoming a working girl. But when he realised it was impossible to persuade me into doing what he expected of me, he tried to trick me into doing a photo shoot that he had already arranged with one of his associates whose name he was reluctant to give but following a succession of arguments it all fell through and his manner towards me changed completely. He became distant and was reluctant to be seen out in public with me, so then of course I realised his expectations of me were far greater than I originally thought. After reading *Little Molly* and *Molly II (Am I Who I should be?)* – the first and second parts of my autobiography, despite the nature of their contents he seemed to take great pleasure in reading certain parts of them over and over again, then planned a very sordid life for me, and a wealthier life for himself.

I recall most evenings were the same, he took a bath around six pm after watering the gardens and as soon as he was dry and settled in his dressing gown, he signed into his laptop and went on sites where he spent half the evening comparing young escort girls to me. After reading my book and taking note that my parents had abandoned me as a small child, I felt he took advantage of my need for affection, giving him all the ammunition he needed to abuse me. I cannot recall at which point I first began to realise that he had no feelings for me, but I noticed a huge difference in him during the month of October 2011; after going home and having a break from him. The short time I spent away was followed by one of our many arguments which often resulted in him becoming aggressive and what I now know to be an act of self-harming. Although I had been staying with him for only four months, I felt like I had spent my whole life with him. The initial few weeks I had spent at Hop Cottage were refreshingly quiet and relaxing, Drew seemed quite caring, despite his admission of lacking confidence around women. He told me that, although he had experienced sexual contact with women before, he had never kissed anyone passionately. It took me a while to figure out that statement and it wasn't until many months later, when he booked himself an escort off the internet, that I learned that the young girls made a point of not kissing or caressing their clients while participating in acts of sexual intercourse; that, I felt, made Drew very cold and demanding towards me. He gave me the impression that he felt nothing but lust each time he got near me and spoke quite frankly about what he expected of me. One thing led to another until it got to the stage where he lured me into taking part in the most sordid sex games that he was generally the narrator of and pieced the most masochistic sex rituals together like any great playwright. His need of such sexual gratification became more apparent to me when I noticed the sudden change in his personality, and I tried to abstain from taking part. The fact he was severely asthmatic did not deter him from frequently demanding high levels of sex from me but by then I was hooked! He studied me and learned from the beginning of our relationship that I suffered from agoraphobia and a severe nervous disposition, so once I had moved into the cottage with him it was difficult for me to leave; so basically, he took advantage of my vulnerability. I have often wondered how I managed to tolerate something like that, but when I think back to the abuse I have suffered and the way it affected me, and my life, it seemed abuse was something I had readily accepted; thinking it was normal! Time passed, and I eventually plucked up the courage to refuse sex with him as often as he demanded, which caused greater problems for me as he began losing patience with me and his personality changed for the worst. In some ways he reminded me of my ex-husband, Smithy, and I frequently told him so, which, surprisingly caused him to alter his ways; for a while anyway! Having read about Smithy in my books, it upset him to think I was comparing him, so I took back what I said and apologised to him. But the fact was, although Drew disliked Smithy's character, his character resembled Smithy's and no matter how much I pointed it out his behaviour around me never completely changed. I had never seen anyone rage and physically beat themselves up like he did, and I feared him the most because of that, as he seemed out of control; and I wondered how long it would be before he turned on me. When I first learnt that he was self-harming I didn't know what to do or say to him, I was frightened to approach him for fear he may attack me; yet I wanted to stop him! I had never witnessed anyone punching and bruising their own face and because it was something I had never experienced before I felt helpless. I didn't understand it and I couldn't for the life of me comprehend his reasons for wanting to damage himself. It took me months to understand why he kept a blood-stained steak knife inside his bedside locker, and I must admit when I first came across it I panicked and wanted to run but instead I decided to confront him about it over the telephone, as I couldn't rest until I knew what it was used for. I wanted to see what reaction he had when I told him I had seen it, before I came face-to-face with him again! My heart wouldn't stop pounding and I could feel sweat running from my brow, as I had already jumped to conclusions and didn't want him to hurt me. Then I gave thought to the blood-stained knife left in the bathroom, surely there must be some logical explanation, I thought! I recall, I sat down on his bed, staring at the stains on the serrated edges of the knife and couldn't for the life of me think of a logical explanation why anyone would keep such a knife in their bedside cabinet. I had been sleeping under the same roof as him for almost eight months before he felt he was able to confide in me, but of course by that time I had already made my own assumptions and began the process of trying to understand why someone who was so successful would self-harm. Most evenings he would take a bath and come out with blood trickling from his feet where he used the knife to physically remove parts of his toe nails, it was something he had been doing since he was a child, he told me. I had trusted him and was persuaded to move from my own home into his beautiful cottage for a more peaceful life, thinking it was the answer to my dreams, somewhere I could write and be happy; that's all I ever asked for. But I was faced with a series of problems that I knew nothing about. I asked myself many times, "What should I do now?" But I had no answers. I feared him, but I had gotten close to him so remained at the cottage and tried my best to understand him. I didn't want to leave and cause him more pain, he had told me so much about his childhood and I knew he was hurting but I didn't know why, as although his life seemed perfect in many ways and free of worry; I wondered if I had got it all wrong.

I had never really looked at myself as being vulnerable before then but having been ill for many years I had reached a stage of my life where I was just trying to improve my own stability, by becoming independent of others. During a period of ten years I had been solely dependent on my carer, Peter Senior, having had a physical and mental breakdown, I had everything done for me and over a period of many years I had no encouragement to try and do anything for myself; so, every muscle in my body had become weak. I found it difficult to concentrate or even think for myself and there was a long period of time I couldn't walk, talk or even eat, basically I lived on water and pureed food that was fed to me from a teaspoon as I could barely swallow even the smallest amount. After ten long years it got to the stage where my dependence on him became a habit rather than a need, so it was at that time I realised if I didn't move away from him I would be forever under his wing and in his debt. There had been times when I wondered if I really needed Peter Senior as much as he needed me, I blamed him for my lack of progress and began to despise him for it, I did all I could to rid myself of him but then guilt set in when people constantly praised him for taking such good care of me; and so I put my own thoughts and welfare aside and tried to appreciate all the good he had done.

Drew on the other hand familiarized himself with my disabilities and once I was accustomed to the cottage he began his moulding procedure. It was easy for him to manipulate me, as I believed him when he told me he loved me and wanted a permanent relationship with me – then he began to lay the foundations. He had a whole lot of expectations and didn't think twice at putting them across. I wondered at that stage if it was really possible for me to meet those expectations, I really didn't think so! He surprised me when he sent me an e-mail of what he expected from me, headed 'Feelings' – it went something like this:

Rosemarie,

This is a first but here goes, over the last few months getting to know you has been a real eye opener for me, I thought I'd seen and done it all, having six pubs, 1,200 tenants and having been a debt collector on some of the roughest estates around here; but your story inspires me. For me in a relationship there has to be a strong physical attraction, she has to have compassion for people, humour in abundance, very stylish but willing to get her hands dirty when needed, generous, a good old-fashioned country girl, brilliant cook, great lover and passionate about, whatever it is we are doing….and that's you. I have had the most incredible highs with you, where I literally think I can take on the world with the confidence you give me. As I have said, I have the confidence to go to the bank and ask for a million quid mortgage and get it but not have the confidence to ask someone like you, out for a drink; strange eh? I have been brutally honest with you in all I have told you and this is the truth; I am the loyalest bloke ever, I am so proud when I am out with you and some might say smug; I suppose in a way I am. People like Eddie and Pete baffle me the way they shout and bawl at you, after reading your books, I should imagine, that is the totally wrong way to treat you; that's why I don't and never will. I know I can help you and you help me but as I have said we need trust, I'd love you to go out with the girls in Peterborough, I can imagine the attention you would get but I know you respect what we have, it would be hard for me but I believe we all need space, if I could have stability and trust with you then I know everything would fall into place. The thing is, now, if I wasn't with you and was with someone else I would be forever comparing them with you, you would come out on top in every aspect, be it clothes, sex, humour, passion, whatever, if we can overcome the problems once and for all; who knows you might even get me down that aisle....

When I first received this from him, I felt rather flattered by his comments but after reading it several times I wondered if he was expecting too much of me. We had only known each other a few months and already I had begun to wonder what he really wanted from me. He was no Arnold Shwarzenegger, yet he brimmed with so much confidence, at times I felt quite inferior at the side of him. He knew every person we came into contact with and during the first few months of our relationship he introduced me to the chosen few, but it became apparent that he was reluctant to take me out with him, particularly when he went out socialising with friends or people he knew. I had already slotted into the familiar pattern of remaining cooped up indoors, cooking, cleaning and generally 'making myself useful' as he so often put it; while he wandered out and around Dover enjoying himself. It wasn't long before the cottage began to feel like a millstone around my neck, as I spent most of my time trying to turn its dreary, cold rooms into the warm homely place that he boasted about before I arrived there. I spent my whole days stacking logs for the wood burner and turning the already beautiful cottage gardens into more spectacular ones. No sooner had I finished one job than he casually mentioned other work that needed doing, knowing I wouldn't refuse… and even suggested I accompanied him to Homebase or B&Q to purchase certain items I would need to carry out specific chores. Washing his clothes, cleaning and cooking were nothing to stacking up logs as high as I could ready for the winter months. I began to feel so isolated and used, but that gave me ample of time to think about all the things that were happening around me, and I began to regret ever going there! It wasn't the first time I had been treated that way and I began to accept that I didn't deserve anything better. I had a general ideal of how men should treat their women but couldn't understand what it was about me that encouraged them to disrespect me, when all I ever did was go out of my way to please them. Over many years I had heard women say, "Treat them mean! Keep them keen!" It was an awful quotation and always refrained from using it, but after meeting Drew I wondered if I was just too nice for my own good. My empathy and kindness were thrown back in my face and I felt used and let down. When I was a child it took me a lot of hard work, sacrifice and empathy to receive respect from someone but as an adult it was like I was carrying an "aura" around me or a label on my forehead saying, "Abuse Me"! I recall my father saying, "If you don't expect, you are rarely disappointed," but respect and honesty were all I ever hoped for – everything else I was capable of doing myself! Up to that stage of my life I had been let down so much that I considered I was either a magnet to those who expected far more from me than they were willing to give, or I was a very bad judge of character.

When I was a young woman I was told my main downfall was being attracted to people who had been disregarded by society and didn't really fit into any characterisation, or the type of person I had to reform before I could be seen out in public with them. My defence to that statement was always the same; I had also met many "upper class people" but never judged anyone by their status, as I had learned from a very young age that there was no class distinction to abuse and neglect!

I had always thought that my demeanour was partly to blame for the way I was treated by other people, as even when I was a teenager I often got into trouble with girls of my own age for no other reason but the way I dressed and carried myself. I was perceived as being wealthy and upper class, but of course I am neither of those! My true character is that I have an abundance of love and warmth, with a caring, sharing nature, willing to take on responsibilities and help anyone in need, as and when it is needed. Having given it some thought I now understand more about the way I felt during my most recent breakdown and the agoraphobia I found so difficult to shake off; it represents everything I have reason to fear: dishonest, manipulating, untrustworthy individuals who spend most of their lives deciphering ways to gain and prosper, using the most unsuspecting, vulnerable people such as myself. Over a period of many years I have wrongly given my trust, only to find that later I have become a target of those who like to abuse and destroy others!

I realised there wasn't much difference between Drew and me, he wasn't stupid or gullible as some people thought. Instead, what I noticed was that his so-called friends and acquaintances used his need for friendship to gain what they could from him and relied on his discretion and occasional good nature. I thought I had met and experienced every type of character during my life, but I realised the quotation 'don't judge a book by its cover!' were the truest words ever spoken. People who knew Drew had mixed opinions of him and the way he obtained his wealth and preyed on the vulnerable, but I found he had been reliant upon his parents and siblings good name and nature to get where he was. And I had supposed it was because of that, the locals, when they were laden with alcohol, were brazen enough to verse their opinion in front of him, and it was only then that I realised he wasn't as well liked as I thought. Early in our relationship I was led to believe, by his closest acquaintances, that he was nothing other than the perfect citizen of Dover, a lot of money exchanged hands between Drew and these people, so I could see why they were loyal to him, and insist on giving him such a good report. Others, whose names remained unknown to me had a very poor opinion of him, and told me so, in fact there were many times when I was warned to get away from him. I recall a small-framed female who was angry enough to approach him when I was out socialising with him, enjoying a Sunday afternoon drink in one of the pubs in Dover. She spieled off such a mouthful of verbal abuse and information regarding his past but I picked up very little of what she said, apart from when she screamed into his face, "Does she know, has he told you?" She blurted out. "Have you told her, Drew?" I focussed on the advice she yelled at me, "Don't trust him! Find someone else! You can do better than him; get away while you can… And demand he tells you, if he doesn't then I will." It was all so confusing, but he reassured me she was a drunk and to take no notice of her. I was absolutely dumbfounded, shocked at the fact that although she was so petite she was angry enough to approach us both and be so upfront with him! She was the first person I had ever seen confront him like that, but even so, she seemingly knew just how far to go before she stormed away muttering to herself angrily. Drew didn't know what to do with himself after that, he turned away in embarrassment and when I asked him about her and what she was referring to he just wouldn't discuss it! By that time, he had read my autobiography and knew almost as much about me as I did. He had already worked out I had not been an academic whiz-kid at school and because of my vulnerability he found he could run rings around me; and proceeded to do exactly that.

I recall him advising Deano, "Be cautious when she's around, she's more observant than most women!" I couldn't understand why he would want to say something like that, then go out of his way to tell me what Deano's response was but I suppose it was that which made me inquisitive and I began to wonder what kind of relationship I had gotten myself into. Drew and

Deano seemed to have one of the closest relationships I had ever observed between two men, they were secretive when I was around, and the atmosphere could have been cut with a knife, so to speak. When I give thought to my past relationships I don't think anyone ever befriended me solely for my own attributes, over a period of four decades I only ever met those who selfishly used my unfortunate circumstances to benefit their own lives – and that really disappointed me as I had hoped that Drew was going to be different but it turned out that even he found it relatively simple to use me. Having prior knowledge that I had been abused as a child and put into care, he summed up relatively early in our relationship that I was more ready to overlook the occasional knockback and abusive treatment, when he considered I had not treated him with the respect and honour he thought he deserved! As a result of being raised in a care home and abused most of my young life, I failed to detect or recognise abuse within my heterosexual relationships and found that I more readily accepted emotional, sexual and physical pain as the norm. I failed to trust my own judgement when I was being verbally attacked, as not having the experience of a normal family home and upbringing I had nothing to compare it with. A life full of pain and misery was all I had ever known; it came alongside invasion of privacy, abusive name-calling, intimidation, violence and even rape. It was about a year before I recognised the tell-tale signs of abuse and because I didn't think I deserved anything better, I put up with being treated that way. It wasn't easy coming to terms with it, in fact I tried ignoring it again and told myself everything would get much better and we would be okay. I kept on trying to be everything he said I should be and because I couldn't explain my thoughts and feelings as well as he could, he became angry and frustrated with me, just like everyone else in my life had done before him. What he failed to absorb and understand was the fact I had not been raised openly amongst normal society, so had never been taught to describe my feelings the same way as he had. I was never taught about relationships, love and affection or how I was supposed to treat others or in fact how they were supposed to treat me! No one had ever shown me how to behave amongst a normal family, in a normal environment, therefore I did not think or behave in a way he and many others perceived as being "normal"!

It was at that stage of my life I began telling myself, 'If aggression, violence and dominance are so readily accepted by our society; then maybe I prefer to be, "an outcast".' Drew lost every ounce of respect for me very quickly and I began to get angry with him because of that, and because of his constant finger-pointing I began seeing only faults in myself, I accepted his constant criticism for my poor communication skills and began thinking even less about myself than I ever did. His pressure tactics became more obvious and he found great pleasure in humiliating me, particularly when he had been out socialising and found himself in a position of being ridiculed by others himself; like he so often was. It seemed those who knew him well took great pleasure in ridiculing him in public bars, knowing he could not retaliate in the same aggressive manner they were using, as it wouldn't have been good for business; so, he took most things on the chin and released his frustration on me when he got home. It would be fair for me to say that on some occasions he was quite sweet, and I remember thinking to myself 'if only you were like this all the time'! The longer I remained with Drew the harder it was for me to leave as at times his personality was lovely, in fact I would go as far to say he portrayed "the perfect gentleman" but it was never very long before he became irritable again. He began to assess me and about nine months into our relationship he issued me with a wad of paperwork that clearly read "Borderline Personality". My initial thought was that he had accepted he may have a problem and had sought help and as a result had been issued with the relevant paperwork, but I was wrong! He began to explain that he thought, I was suffering from a Cognitive Personality Disorder and he had taken the liberty to speak with an associate who managed to obtain the relevant paperwork that explained what Cognitive Personality Disorder was, and how it affects a person who was suffering from it. I was shocked at his insinuation and although I accepted the paperwork, I did so only to prevent him from reacting badly if I didn't. As I reluctantly glanced over the paperwork and began to read it to myself, he ordered me to read it out loud. I began at the head of the page not really knowing if I was going to understand what I was reading but I did as he said and read it out loud… It went something like this – "Borderline Personality is a disorder of emotion and behaviour regulation. The disorder might be thought of as a defect in the individual's internal ability to regulate emotional intensity and the behaviours that result. As a result, the person with Borderline Personality Disorder is periodically overwhelmed by abnormally intense emotions that drive him/her to seek relief".

It went on and on but the literature that most inter-ested me was the part he pointed out to me and said he was convinced it most resembled my personality. He looked across at me as if he was monitoring my reaction to it all, but I gave him no indication to the way I felt and tried hard not to become emotional over his disheartening suggestion that I needed to seek psychiatric help. The fact that his twenty-four-year-old son was apparently registered with STEPPS (a Reinforcement Team) who helped people with this kind of illness didn't seem to register; it was only after he gave me an A4 sheet of paper which STEPPS had labelled "Common negative (unhelpful) filters" which he said most described me.

I read from 1 to 10…

Connection to others

1. Emotional Deprivation "I'll never get the love I need".

You believe that your important needs, e.g. affection, protection, caring, will not be met by others. People with this filter have difficulty trusting others, do not easily accept assistance from others and appear very independent, even aloof. This filter may have begun when someone very important to you e.g. a parent did not provide for your needs.

Basic Safety

2. Abandonment "Please don't leave me".

You believe that anyone who comes to you will eventually leave you. To avoid the pain of feeling abandoned, people with this filter avoid close relationships, and or purposely (or subconsciously) do something to cause a relationship to end before the other person ends it. This filter may have developed due to a past significant loss or having been frequently left alone for extended periods of time, especially during childhood.

Mistrust "I can't trust you"

3. You believe others cannot be trusted… Those others will eventually take advantage of or abuse you in some way. People with this filter expect others to hurt, cheat, manipulate, lie, or put them down. Any hurt is seen as intentional. People with this filter may think of attacking the other person first or put great effort into revenge. This filter may follow severe or ongoing abuse or unfair treatment from significant person such as a parent.

Self-esteem

4. Defectiveness/social undesirability, "I'm worthless". "I don't fit in". You believe that you are different from other people, flawed, bad, inferior, and socially undesirable and that, if you let others get to know you, they will find out. This often leads to a strong sense of shame. People with this filter may be hypersensitive to criticism, rejection and blame, and are self-conscious and insecure around others. This filter may result from ongoing rejection by significant others such as parents or peers.

Fail to achieve.

5. "I feel like I am such a failure". You believe you are not capable of performing as well as your peers in areas such as work, education or sport. People with this filter may feel stupid, useless, untalented or ignorant and others do not try to achieve because they believe they will fail.

Autonomy/independence

6. Vulnerability to harm and illness, "Catastrophe is about to strike". You believe that you are on the verge of experiencing a major random catastrophe (financial, natural, medical, criminal etc.) No matter how well things may be going, you expect trouble. You believe that you can't handle life's difficulties. People with this filter may take excessive precautions to protect themselves. They may avoid pleasant activities to avoid the pain of the hurt they believe will soon occur. Some people with this filter rely on others excessively for help such as making decisions or starting something new. This filter may have started after a significant trauma such as an illness or the loss of an important person.

Focus on Others

7. Self-sacrifice, "Other people are more important than me and must be put first".

You believe that you must sacrifice your own needs in order to help others. People with this filter feel guilty when they pay attention to their own needs. To avoid this guilt, they put others needs ahead of their own. Helping others may give them a sense of identity. This filter often leads to a sense that one's own needs are not being met and they resent those they are taking care of. Some people alternate between self-sacrifice and entitlement. This filter may be related to having excessive demands placed on you, especially during childhood.

8. Subjugation, "I'll always do it your way".

You believe you must submit to others in order to avoid negative consequences. You surrender control over your behaviour, emotional expression and decisions because you feel pressurised by others. People with this filter often fear that others will get angry or reject them if they don't submit. They may believe that their own desires, opinions and feelings are not valid or important. People with this filter are excessively accommodating and may be hypersensitive to feeling trapped. Anger is often suppressed when this filter is active. This filter may start when a person is constantly invalidated and/ or made dependent on another.

Self-expression

9. Unrelenting standard "Nothing I do is ever quite good enough".

You believe whatever you do is not quite good enough, not acceptable. You believe that you must meet excessively high perfectionistic standards of behaviour and perform in order to avoid criticism (from yourself and others). People with this filter may place excessive emphasis on status, wealth, and power at the expense of relationships, health and happiness. People with this filter often have trouble slowing down, feel pressurised and are very critical of themselves and others. This filter may be rooted in perfectionistic standards of parents and peers.

Realistic Limits

10. Entitlement "I can have whatever I want". You believe that you should be able to do, say or have whatever you want right now, regardless of whether it hurts others or seems unreasonable to them. Others (and the world in general) owe you. People with this filter have an excessive tendency to assert their power,

force their point of view on, or control others. People with this filter may be very demanding and self-focused and are often unaware of the long-term cost of alienating other people. This filter may develop as a response to negative life experiences.

I reluctantly glanced over both sides of the A4 page that he insisted I read as he randomly bought to my attention filters 1, 2, 3, 4, 5, 7, 8 and 9 that I noticed he had marked with a small cross on the left-hand side of each paragraph. As I studied each paragraph, I repeatedly referred to the title of the informative page, 'Common Negative (unhelpful) filters' then took notes of the information given at the foot of the page which read: 'Adapted from, *Jeffrey Young's Cognitive Therapy for Personality Disorders. A Schema-Focused Approach*, 1999' which at that point meant very little to me – apart from realising that after ten months of failing to convince me that I was out of control and almost beyond help, Drew tried a different approach by producing a copy of his twenty-four-year-old son's information and note pack from the 'STEPPS' programme that he said his son was attending. Having only Drew's word for the reasons for this, I open-mindedly listened to all the information he was so readily willing to inform me of, but always bearing in mind that Drew was this boy's biological father and had, in my opinion, afforded him a life no better than my own.

I had noticed from the onset of mine and Drew's relationship that there were severe flaws in his personality and although he seemed slightly immature a lot of the time, at other times he surprised me – how intellectual he could be and how he portrayed a more mature role when he was around influential people. I read the information over and over again, taking time to compare the notes first with my own personality and then Drew's. Admittedly, I recognised traits of my own personality within the filters; as must most of us would who have taken the time to read through it. However, I found it particularly interesting that a large percentage of it resembled Drew's personality but also noticed how he was so reluctant to admit that the similarity between him and the filters was more detectable than in either me or his son. I found that paragraph 10 adequately described Drew's character and read through it more than once just to try and get a clear understanding of it. It was true, Drew did think he was entitled to do, say or have whatever he wanted, even if and when it hurt other people; no matter how unreasonable it may have seemed to them. For some strange reason he was of the opinion that everyone in the world owed him something and as it described: "The people with this filter did have an excessive tendency to assert their power, force their point of view on, and control others", just as Drew did with me. He was typically very demanding and self-focussed and what I really found ironic was that it accurately described the obvious unawareness of his unpredictable, unfriendly and aggressive behaviour. Drew's reason for supplying me with all this informative paperwork was to educate me about the personality disorder he thought that I suffered from. He insisted that I approached my GP Dr Wilson to discuss the possibility of me having a serious borderline personality disorder and even told me to take the list of described filters with me so the doctors could diagnose it properly. Having ticked most of the filters he made it obvious to me that he was convinced I was as disturbed as he thought his son was. He repeatedly told me there was no other way and that he believed I needed medication to rectify the problem. He had this uncanny way of convincing me that I was far from normal and often described me as being hypersensitive to criticism which he thought was uncalled for. I recognised he had some kind of personality disorder so I basically cowed down to him just to lessen the frequency of his aggressive outbursts. The fact that I had once again become isolated didn't seem to bother him, in fact the times that he left me alone in the cottage became more frequent and for longer periods. He readily accepted the fact that I suffered from agoraphobia and knew I couldn't go out alone as the terrible fear of large open spaces and crowds was often more than I could bear; but being left alone to suffer in silence just added to my fears and isolated me even more. By choosing to go out socialising and entertaining himself, while I remained at the cottage working on the list of "things to do" he regularly prepared for me, caused me to doubt his feelings for me and I spent most of my time working and wondering what his intentions were. On the many occasions I withdrew money from my bank he would ask me to accompany him to do the food shopping and re-stock the supply of beers and wines he kept, knowing his intention was to get me to pay for it. He had this uncanny way of moving away from the checkout and often left the store before we reached the tills and I was left to struggle to unload and pack everything from the heavily loaded trolley. It more or less worked every time we visited food, clothing or hardware stores, but even when I realised what he was doing, I was far too nervous to mention it or even say no. Drew knew how to manipulate people but I felt he particularly enjoyed manipulating me! I had told him that I enjoyed visiting Dover Castle with friends before I met him, it wasn't a very busy period and I found being out with friends helped me and I handled the open space quite well. And although Drew occasionally made an effort to take me there, he focussed more on seaside resorts, garden centres and historic buildings that seemed to be his speciality, most of which we visited at my expense – and again I was too gullible to say no. It was towards the end of our relationship before I accepted the fact he was just using me, taking as much as he could as often as he could; it seemed I was just one more, unsuspecting, vulnerable individual who he took pleasure in manipulating. It cost me heavily; just to be treated abusively by him. All I expected from people was to be treated with the upmost respect and decency, the same way I treated them, but I struggled to find anyone who respected me enough to treat me as they expected to be treated.

I've always been the type of person to defend myself when I felt threatened and it seemed there was always someone who wanted to be in control of me and expected to push me around without any comeback; but that wasn't the way I was taught! The only time Drew showed appreciation or respect for me was when I worked my butt off for him, either keeping the cottage and its gardens cleaned and maintained or decorating and cleaning out the properties he owned when they became vacant. He often told me he couldn't do anything quite as well as anyone else and seemed to rely on people to do much of the work for him, as he was convinced others could do it better; something I believe was drilled into his head when he was a child. He had a very low opinion of himself most of the time and sought praise for what I considered to be childlike activities that he succeeded in. During the times he didn't succeed he became angry very quickly and found it difficult to control his temper, but he never really opened up to tell me why he responded that way. He spoke very highly about his mother and repeatedly told me how lovely she was. He had hoped to find someone just like her and said I was the person who fit that bill. As he described her, I formed a picture in my mind of a very petite, considerate person who wasn't only physically attractive but a dedicated mother who would do anything for her family. He made it very clear to me that his upbringing was far superior to mine and even arranged for me to watch one of their long family videos which his eldest brother filmed over many years of happy family life. Having already read, *Little Molly* and *Molly II (Am I Who I Should Be?)* he knew that my life had no resemblance to his own, and their perfect family get-togethers and sentimental moments were alien to me. But it wasn't until their two-hour long film had finished that he expressed concern for my feelings and the way I felt while watching it. My eyes had filled with tears so many times, while the film ran through some of their happiest moments and Christmas at its best, scenes I had dreamt about when I was a little girl and yet I loved watching it! It gave me a realistic idea of what normal family life was about and I felt really happy for him, even so I could not understand why he had developed such strange tendencies when he had been raised so well. I wondered if he wasn't as open and honest about his upbringing, so I tried to encourage him to talk about the members of his family he was estranged from; but nothing materialised from it!

I recall Christmas 2011 when he practised deceiving me and began a series of argumentative scenes, which eventually developed into physical brawls. Drew was a good thirty stone in weight and measured fifty-four inches around his chest, not the size of a man I would have picked a fight with, but as he was very provoking it always seemed to have the same result, he became violently aggressive and self-harmed and I would get scared and leave him alone at the cottage; only to return a few days later when he had calmed down. I never wanted to leave him because, despite all of his faults, I loved him dearly and knew for a fact that if he could have changed his habits I would have stayed with him for the rest of my life. I was never able to understand what caused him to be like he was, but gradually as he spoke about certain things that had happened during his life he eventually, after a lot of coaxing, recalled childhood memories that made me think; perhaps he did not have the best childhood after all! He confessed that his school days were not the best; he had suffered lots of embarrassing moments and was often ridiculed by other children. As far as I understood, even his older brother taunted him with sarcastic comments and insulting remarks about his mental and physical abilities, so it seemed Drew had been convinced from a young age that he wasn't as sensible or as academically sound as his older brother Garry and was often told by Garry himself that he was a "weirdo" – and throughout his school days convinced Drew that he was far from normal. He laughed half-heartedly and tried to convince me that he took it all in good part, but beneath that strange, childlike grin he had I saw a little boy in him, just crying out for someone to believe in him. It was easy for me to forget that this giant size of a man once had a warm and tender heart, but he had been raised to believe he was nothing but a "weirdo" who was second best to everyone.

—∞—

CHAPTER 9

Cause to Feel Shame

There are a lot of myths around domestic abuse. It is often thought to be a working-class problem; however, women of all social classes, races and nationalities suffer abuse of all types. The cause can be income, level of education, age, religion, sexuality, disability, mental health, marital status or even occupation – and the list goes on. While I was at Drew's I began to study every-one woman I came into contact with, I wondered if they were going through the same thing I was going through but most of them seemed happy and relaxed; they looked nothing like I felt inside. There was a time when I began to wonder if I looked like an "abused woman", I even questioned my own thoughts and asked myself, what is abuse, could it be that my definition of abuse is not correct? Then I began to think about my childhood and asked myself, 'did I ever see myself as a victim, was it obvious to other people?' The answer of course; was no! I never saw myself as a victim; simply because I didn't understand I was being abused. Although we have progressed since the 1960s, when I was abused as a little girl, I don't think many of us who have suffered and still suffer from abuse recognise it as such, as it is seldom openly spoken about, and as far as I know there are very few awareness campaigns to try and help to rectify the problem of abuse. I have very often asked myself, is it normal for a person to be in control of another? Maybe I expect too much from life so deserve to be treated abusively.... But of course, no one deserves to be treated abusively! All of these horrible thoughts have run through my mind until I have become so mixed up and confused that all I wanted to do was escape from those most likely to harm me. I have seldom met anyone who really understood about such things and cared enough to get to know me, so I have made very few friends during my life and although I have always accepted responsibility for that, I honestly think the reason for it was because I never found anyone who had the empathy or understanding that an "abused" person really needed. Meeting people and making friends never felt comfortable and I never relaxed around them, so I gave the wrong impression and put out the wrong kind of vibes, in such a way that I portrayed I just didn't care and could take them or leave them. Then that created other problems within my relationships and led to further abuse and although I knew this kind of thing happened, I thought it was totally normal. For the largest part of my life I have felt miserable, I lost my self-esteem and believed I wasn't worth the shoes I stood up in. Throughout our relationship, Drew constantly told me that he loved me and like a fool I believed him, he said it with so much sincerity in his voice I am sure anyone would have believed him; but during those awful times when he switched to the ogre part of his personality it seemed like he hated me. I tried to understand what was going on between us, but he regularly insinuated it was all happening because of the abuse I had suffered as a child, I failed to understand what he meant by that as it didn't explain why he treated me the way he did!

I often thought I should pack my bags and leave while he was out socialising, but I had never been a quitter, so I stupidly tried to persevere with the relationship for as long as I could. In the back of my mind was the thought that he might change, and things would get better, but when all night long, heated discussions failed I reverted to writing things down that I needed to say to him, as amongst all the trauma I forgot most of what was important and even after trying to communicate with him in that way, I failed. He did not understand how I felt about living my life around him, as that's all I seemed to do – live my life around him! I recall one particular incident, it was the early hours of the morning when he staggered through the back door, slurring his words and tugging clumsily at his very expensive, black leather jacket. After struggling to remove it from his back, after several minutes it fell to the floor as he lost his grip of it. He stepped to one side as he attempted to pick it up but staggered all over the place, this was a sign he had been drinking heavily and although he seemed in a relatively good mood, I sensed he had something on his mind when he didn't put his arms around me like he usually did when he was drunk, and I thought, not again! He staggered into the lounge and through to the bathroom and after a sudden clatter of what could only be shampoo and deodorant canisters falling to the floor, I heard him urinate and flush the toilet before he staggered back out and into the lounge, where he clumsily stoked up the burner with logs. He spoke very few words before he crashed heavily into one of the easy chairs in the corner of the room and began an episode of intimidating speeches and finished by very demandingly saying: "Now it's your turn!" He enjoyed putting me on the spot. Once he realised my level of vocabulary did not match his, he seemed to revel in the fact that it embarrassed me when I didn't understand some of the words he used, and I was too nervous to speak my mind. He got angry with me before I would even attempt to converse with him, I suppose that was my stubborn streak, but my words would not flow from my mouth, the same way his did from his mouth and the result was always the same, he became more angry and I got more upset. Then he left me crying on the sofa, while he staggered down the long hall way to his bedroom in an attempt to get into bed. Renowned for standing my ground, I always tried to demonstrate a show of strength to obtain respect and was reluctant to join him while he was in a bad mood, and often chose to sleep on the sofa until he had sobered up. Occasionally he made his way back to the lounge, solely to order me to bed with him but it didn't always work out the way he expected it to! I do recall, during the long winter months when the snow lay thick on the ground, we burned a tremendous number of logs and the fire would eventually burn its way out and I appreciated the fact he took the time and effort to come and wake me, as the hard leather sofa was cold and uncomfortable.

The temperature in the cottage dropped significantly low and rather than him think I was weak, I shivered with cold as I tried to sleep. The eighteenth century cottage was a beautiful looking place, but it was so cold and draughty, not at all like the modern buildings of today. The central heating system was always breaking down and even after Drew sent for Deano to repair it, it was never too long before it was out of action again. Drew didn't feel the cold like I did and could never understand why I constantly complained about it; when I did he suggested I wrapped myself up with one of the throws he used to spread on the wooden floor to lay on, or the quilt off his bed. This is when I particularly regret not keeping to the arrangements we initially made before I went to stay there, where I was offered a bedroom of my own and an office to write my books, I suppose it would be fair to say it was a mistake we both made. When Drew wasn't working or out socialising he spent hour upon hour laid belly down on the hard wooden floor, tip-tapping away at what remained of the keys on his laptop, that was so damaged and worse for wear it was a wonder it worked at all; but I noticed it functioned well enough for him to spend most of his time searching through women's profiles until he came across one that he was attracted too, then after thoroughly vetting them, sent them a friend request. There was so much more to him than I had ever imagined, and I just couldn't get my head around all the weird things he did. His life touched so many other people's lives and although he denied having many sexual partners or encounters, I eventually found out that he lied about that too. I was puzzled and was left feeling uncertain most of the time, as so many people came in and out of his life, I often thought to myself: 'What the hell am I doing with him?' Despite the nature of the abuse I had suffered and the horrible life I had encountered, I just felt I wasn't experienced enough for a man like him. Although I had experienced many things, I realised there was a lot more to life than I had ever envisaged, it seemed he had so much going on. Although at the beginning of our relationship he spent much of his time with me, because of his lack of trust in most people, he would not confide in me the same way he confided in Deano, which in turn made me mistrust him. Drew informed me that he had always experienced difficulty in approaching women, for instance when he was out socialising he said he felt inferior to a lot of people. He had reached the age of fifty and confessed he had never kissed a woman passionately before he kissed me. I found it very difficult to believe, as he had previously told me about several relationships he had supposingly experienced, none that I would have considered as, "the norm!" He often spoke about a girl named Fiona who he had known for a number of years, I believe he somehow became her guardian when she was around the age of fourteen but said she had become reliant on drugs and was eventually committed to hospital. He said she had become too ill to survive amongst society and pursued him when she got out. I met her only on one occasion when she approached us at a public bar in Dover, I didn't know her but was shocked when she tried to tell me something in front of him and he became angry, and stood with his back to her. He made it obvious to me that he was blocking her view of me. He immediately told me to drink up and grabbed my arm and escorted me out of the pub, I have never forgotten that she looked like me and wore her hair the same way I wore mine; but I never saw her again! She was a fraction of my age, no more than thirty I would say and despite the fact I asked him about her he never mentioned her after that. The longest heterosexual relationship he had ever experienced was with one of his business partners, Sharon, who lived with him for the best part of seven years, yet he informed me that even his relationship with her wasn't what it should have been, after a couple of years of living together they decided to sleep in separate rooms and eventually separated when she began having an affair with another man. Drew was very evasive regarding their breakup and despite my inquisitiveness he would not confide in me enough to tell me how she had managed to obtain a reasonably successful business in Dover and had become a partner in some of the properties he owned.

When I first met him, he seemed to trust me implicitly but gradually over a few months he stopped confiding in me and became more like a stranger than anything else. He was forever picking arguments with me and although I tried my utmost to please him, in many ways I think I tried too hard as he got accustomed to me running around after him, trying to please him so he expected it! It got to the stage where I just couldn't give him any more than I was giving, and I couldn't love him anymore than I did, yet he pushed for more until I was so exhausted, I felt completely drained. It was at that stage of our relationship he began going out a lot more, leaving me alone in the cottage most days and evenings too. He was out socialising and having fun while I cleaned the cottage or helped maintain the gardens for him. I took orders from him to bathe and prepare myself ready for him when he came home; a regular demand that he made every night. Having had a severely abusive childhood and lifelong existence, where abuse seemed to be just a natural way of life there seemed no getting away from it. I was once told by a psychologist that it was possible I was naturally drawn to characters similar to the ones who had abused me when I was a child growing up, but I was reluctant to accept that, as I had known some very gentle, loving men who I hold a great amount of respect for. When Drew occasionally managed to drag himself away from his work and regular social life to spend a little time with me, the highlight of the day was for me to accompany him to Canterbury in search of retail lingerie, shops typical of Ann Summers, to purchase aids and seductive clothing to make his sex life "out of the ordinary" he said. This was when I realised our relationship was not a loving one and was never going to be, in fact it was all about his gratification, I wanted it to be so much more than that, but it seemed he was just another guy using me. I stuck it out hoping I was wrong, but things just gradually got worse. It was at this stage of our relationship that I realised his sex drive was far from normal and his persistent demands for sex no longer felt complimentary, in fact his emotional release of sexual frustration became quite frightening, especially when I told him I was too tired or showed reluctance to participate. I hadn't witnessed such frightening emotions since I was a child, his frustration and involuntary spasms I can only presume were caused by his great expectancy. Very often he poured out a large gin and tonic from what he referred to as his 'alcoholic stash' and handed it to me in a very large glass, presumably to make it look smaller than the amount it really was, and coaxed me into drinking it. I had been taking prescription medication for many years and did not consume alcohol very often so became drunk very quickly, but it wasn't until much later that I realised it gave him the opportunity to take advantage of me while I was intoxicated. I don't quite remember when it first became apparent to me that he couldn't control his sex drive, but what I can recall is that he became forceful to the extent that my consent was no longer deemed necessary and he voluntarily told me he had sexually invaded my body on occasions while I had been sleeping. I wasn't aware of that until the day he went berserk and I had to make an emergency call to the Kent police to obtain protection from him. Since the police enquiries I have been informed by them that the medication I was on would have exaggerated the strength of the alcohol, therefore I would have been unfit to give sexual consent anyway; but that was another story.

—ɱ—

CHAPTER 10

A Glimpse of Reality

I wasn't quite sure what to make of my life; I was living in a world where everything seemed to be chaotic and in disarray. Having left Market Deeping, I was trying to come to terms with the changes I had made to my life and repeatedly told myself, 'it was all for the best.' But then I wondered, who was I trying to convince? At the age of fifty-three I was still trying to find happiness but asked myself, 'does it really exist?' As I relaxed to the back of my chair, I clasped my hands together as I sat and wondered what it would take to make me happy, would it be showering me with the finer things of life or possibly something a little more simple, like sitting peacefully at my desk gazing through the clouded glass windows admiring the beautiful array of pink, white and blue blossoms that flourished amongst the vibrant green ferns that decorated the hedgerows? Might it be possible that I won't find happiness amongst man himself but in and amongst other living things, far more beautiful... I have yet to learn! As I sat listening to the hypnotic, hoarse voice of Rod Stewart coming across my PC, singing songs that signified the way I was feeling: *Broken Arrow*, *The First Cut Is the Deepest* and *All for Love*, the words of each one of those songs cut deep into my soul as I sat nursing yet another lonely hour, wishing that my life had been different. No matter how I tried to change things, I sank deeper and deeper into a state of morbid anxiety, thinking only of the unpleasant day to day events that seemed to surround me. I asked myself, was my life really worth living? When my children were small I used to convince myself that it was all worth it because at least my children needed me but at that particular moment I wasn't so sure my life meant anything to anybody. I wondered if the heartache would ever come to an end, if not that night, some other night maybe. I had exchanged the office where I wrote *Little Molly* and *Molly II* for a tiny room without a view, at the rear of Drew's' beautiful cottage. I had fallen in love with the cottage, but I wasn't happy. I recall, my mother told me, early on in my life that I allowed my heart to rule my head and, in her opinion, where I went wrong in my relationships. I was young and foolish back then so chose what little advice of hers I adhered too, and have met with lots of problems as a result of that! Mother died prior to me meeting Drew and I found myself wishing that she had lived longer, I missed her terribly and felt saddened by the fact that I never told her how much I really loved her. Despite my upbringing and the differences that developed between us, Mother and I eventually became quite close, we tried to put all the sad and heart-breaking memories behind us and focussed on the good times; it seemed we coped better that way! If only I'd have realised how much it was going to hurt when she died I would have spent more time with her, as there was so much more to her than any of us knew, so much had been left unsaid. Apart from the heartbreak I experienced over the loss of my children when I was a young mother, I had felt no pain like the pain I felt when I was told that her life was over; I was truly devastated! I sat and wondered what I would have done had she still been alive. Would I have confided in her and perhaps told her everything, or would I once again be sat alone, wondering why I allowed myself to get caught up in another unstable relationship, with a man who wouldn't have even given me a second glance if he'd have known what heart-rending complications I came with.

I had hoped the relationship between me and Drew would get better in time, but I felt totally beat, there was something amiss and I wondered if I ever had 'float his boat', a term he used for being desirable. I had carefully studied this man and I must admit he was not a bit like any other person I had ever met. I watched and listened to everything he did and said and was absolutely certain that at times he didn't even know what to make of his own life let alone mine. He informed me that he was normally a very happy person, but I asked him, "happy or just stuck?" I figured he could only live the kind of life he had previously mapped out for himself. When I looked into his eyes I did not see happy, I saw sad and lonely, without 'true friends'. Out of all of the acquaintances he had, I never met any who didn't either earn a living from him or owe him something. After almost five months I had met no one, apart from his parents, who really cared for him, no one who could honestly say they wanted nothing more from him than to be his true and loyal friend. It seemed to me that he paid a heavy price for everything, even friendship. I'm certain he could have had a far happier life, but he kept lots of people in tow, people who owed him money but had no real means or intentions of paying him back and then of course they remained at his beck and call. I believed he enjoyed being in control of them until such time they had paid off their debts. His neighbour, Amid, was also one of Drew's tenants who gambled away his money and often struggled to pay his rent, sometimes owing Drew months at a time, but still, Amid paid the price in many ways. I had suspicion that Drew was sweet on Amid's wife, Katrina, as he had often confided in me and said, "She shouldn't be with him!" Her five-year-old daughter and her two sons had developed a somewhat close relationship with Drew as it seemed he played a very significant part in their lives. Sometimes I pointed it out to him, because I couldn't get my head around the fact that he committed himself with such dedication to both Katrina and the kids, yet he either failed to recognise it himself or thought I was totally naïve. When I and Drew eventually split up I returned to my own home in Market Deeping, as in the short time we were together I noticed many changes in him, where he used to confide and put his trust in me, he seemed to become morbid and distant. By the time Christmas came around I felt as miserable as he looked, as he spent most of his time gazing through the cottage windows across at Amid and Katrina's home. I repeatedly asked him if he wanted me to leave the cottage and told him I could not live with the atmosphere he was creating but he was adamant he wanted me to stay which threw my life into turmoil; I felt so confused I really didn't know what to do for the best. But time moved on and It became more apparent to me that I really should have left much sooner and saved us both a tremendous amount of heartache and pain!

—⁂—

ᴄʜᴀᴘᴛᴇʀ 11

Trying to Get My Life Back

July 13 2015. I began writing from where I left off the year before; it seemed ironic that the last time I wrote anything in *Molly III* was July 14 2014. I had made notes but not entered anything on my laptop as if time had stood still and yet so much had happened during that year. Returning to Market Deeping wasn't really something I had expected to do but as usual I picked up the pieces of yet another broken relationship and moved on as quickly as I could.

As I had only passed my driving test a few weeks before, I found the long drive from Market Deeping to Chesterfield quite daunting, although some parts of the two-hour journey seemed to relax me, I became quite tense when I entered the A1 and the dual carriageway. What seemed to be a very long haul finally came to an end when I arrived at the Queen's Park in Chesterfield, Derbyshire where I had arranged to meet George, someone I hadn't seen or heard from for twenty or so years. I had a very clear memory of George. Although Martin Lawrence was his real name, for whatever reason his family nicknamed him George when he was quite young, and the name stuck, apart from those close to him and family members not many outsiders seem to be aware of it. I first met George in Chesterfield when I was around twenty-seven and lived with my eldest son, Ian, who was about seven years old at that time and my daughter, Cheniel, who was just a toddler. I had been through hell and back before George and I met, and apart from telling him a little about the person I feared the most, my abuser John Wass, I told him very little about myself. My initial impression of George was that he was seemingly very shy and wasn't the type of person I would normally confide in, but I recall telling him early on in our relationship about John Wass. I remember thinking to myself that he might not see me again after I had divulged the facts about the abuse, but I wanted to be open and upfront with him, I didn't want anything to stand in the way of us getting on and honesty was my motto – so I told him as much as dared about our family background. He listened and took everything in his stride a lot easier than I thought he would. I didn't think he truly understood when I told him I was nervous of my brother, he had never experienced anything remotely similar to the abuse I had suffered, so how could he? George was a very naïve person who had been raised in a very caring and sheltered home, with middle to upper class parents but I enjoyed listening to the stories he told about his mum, Joan, and his father, Frank, as his upbringing couldn't have been any further apart from mine; so, I loved to hear about his family. His two older brothers, Peter and Brian, were always in the picture, a great comparison to my own brothers and it was obvious to me at that time that George looked up to them. Although I met Brian soon after meeting George I didn't meet Peter until Christmas 2013. Unlike his brothers, George's demeanour was rather unusual, and I couldn't figure him out as easily as other men I had known in the past. I learned so much about him and was mesmerised by the wonderful stories and adventures of his travels around Australia, and literally fell in love with the music he played on the old piano I bought him for his birthday. He was such a quiet and reserved man with the semblance of a very chilled 60s hippy, and after meeting his father, Frank, it was obvious to me that the beautiful calm mannerisms George had acquired came from his father. I hadn't known George long before he asked me to marry him and I needed no time to think about it before accepting as he had all the qualities that I liked. It was obvious to me that we had been raised totally different but still, the following week, he whisked me down to Surrey to tell his parents we were getting married. His father looked shell-shocked but George said he knew his father was pleased for us, as he always thought George would never get married! Frank was a well-built, ageing gentleman and I could see a resemblance to him in George but there was so much more that I noticed about Frank. I saw similarities in Frank and me, although our worlds seemed so far apart, his persona seemed more or less identical to mine. It wasn't unusual for me, even at the tender age of twenty-seven to have, what was later described by my counsellor, a kind of sixth sense which helped me to detect danger when I was a child. Despite being too young to prevent abuse from taking place, I had, on occasions, managed to hide away and prevent the amount of times it happened to me. I sensed that Frank had deep emotions locked inside of him just crying to get out and I surmised he hadn't been able to unload to anyone. It was obvious to me that he had built a similar protective barrier around himself, just as I had, and eye to eye contact was practically non-existent. The only tell-tale signs of him being pleased at George's unexpected news of our getting married was a firm hand shake and a squeeze of George's forearm as they both strolled casually down the garden path discussing it.

George's mum seemed in a kind of intermittent world, running around as if time was against her. She made it very clear to both George and I, in her swanky high class manner, that we had arrived far later than she had anticipated and showed no embarrassment in being too abrupt about it! It had been a very long car journey, from Chesterfield to Surrey and both George and I were very tired. I was hungry, but it seemed George and his parents were more interested in alcoholic refreshments rather than food, I was a soft drinks person myself and rarely drank alcohol so managed without it. I enjoyed food of any description and, although I had always been relatively slender, when I felt the pangs of hunger I got to the point where I could think of nothing else, so I always tried to avoid becoming too hungry! If my memory serves me right, George's mum had planned to give us a meal when we arrived but because we arrived at their home much later than expected it was no longer available to us, as they had no way or means of keeping it warm. I remember being so shy and withdrawn I wouldn't ask for anything so remained hungry all day. That evening seemed a long drawn out one, I felt uncomfortable and embarrassed at the fact that my stomach kept on rumbling while listening to George's mum, who made it very clear to me that she wore the trousers; in fact, her husband Frank seemed to have no authority over anything at all. I was rather pleased when George announced he would like to visit the wife of one of his best friends, although he knew that her husband wouldn't be there he wanted me to meet her and I was kind of glad to get away, just for a breather. Afterwards, George suggested going to his local pub for a drink and then on to a restaurant for a meal, but the meal never materialised, and the evening ended up a bit of a disaster when we had to rush around the town in the dark, searching for a place to eat. Luckily, we came across an, Indian takeaway where George asked me if I liked curry. Apart from my local chip shop in Chesterfield, I had never experienced Indian food at its best, so I replied, "Yes I do!" without knowing what I was letting myself in for. I had waited so long for something to eat, at that moment in time I felt very grateful for anything he offered, but when he ordered two portions of a hot vindaloo that was far too hot for me to swallow I went to bed hungry!

The following day we accompanied his parents to the Bowls Club where they had become officiated members, they were very well known and were communicative with everyone who was there. It was at times like that I was grateful for the Outrake's input in my life. The Outrake Children's home at Little Longstone in Derbyshire was the place I was raised and had mixed thoughts about, sometimes I remembered only the cruelty that took place there and had never forgotten the bellowing of our voices as they echoed throughout the house while we were being flogged. I developed a nervous disposition and had considered that place responsible for the ruination of, not only my childhood, but my siblings and many other children's too; in fact, all those who had been placed there during my stay! Yet at other times I wondered if I had judged the staff too harshly and ought to be grateful for the good it did me. Since I wrote the first part of my auto-biography *Little Molly*, I have had the pleasure of meeting so many people from my past and realise that the staff's strict regime and untrained input to our care instilled one of two things... Hatred, with an outgoing, glad to be free, rebellious characteristic, or, the shy, institutionalised her-mit-type characteristic... The latter, I would say, fitted my own personality for which I feel somewhat grateful, as I suppose my inability to socialise like any normal person has protected me from many. Admittedly, I have met the occasional undesirable lover... But once I realised they were a bad influence the relationships never lasted and if they were abusive towards me I always sought help. I consider my distinctions to be a trait of the Outrake Children's Home. I could have followed a different path and weakened at some of the most difficult times of my life, where I occasionally struggled to remain dignified, but I stand with my back straight and my head held high, as I feel I have done our care system justice! I am not proud of being raised within the care homes, but I am proud that I survived all that was thrown at me and still look and speak respectfully... and for that, I only have myself to thank!

I recall I had to make a conscious effort to remember what time I was supposed to meet George at the Queen's Park in Chesterfield. Since I had suffered a breakdown I found it even more difficult to remember things relating to numbers, a condition similar to that which I had suf-fered as a child, which caused hardship in learning – one more problem I had got my head around. I arrived in good time and parked my car just outside the gates, at the top entrance of the park, and nervously walked through the beautiful well-kept gardens and down towards the bridge, where I could see people walking. My eyes immediately focussed on a gentleman dressed in a light-coloured suit and what looked like a trilby perched on top of his head. He stood out from the crowd, not the tidiest of men by any means but I was never one to judge a book by its cover! As I walked nervously towards him, I tried to act cool and confident but when I realised it was George, my heart raced and the butterflies in my stomach just would not settle. As we came face-to-face I noticed lots of physical changes had occurred over the years and my first impression was that life hadn't been kind to him. His face was the first thing I focussed upon as he seemed to have an obvious, maroon-tinged complexion with patches of dull yellowing on his cheeks and his brows, broken veins extended themselves to cover his roman shaped nose which were dark purple in colour. I leaned forward to hug him and said, "Hiya Georgie!" But the stench on his clothing was quite overpowering, one that I recognised, and I remembered he never did wear antiperspirant or deodorant, and was never open to persuasion. Just for a few moments I stood in front of him gazing at his very unusual and noticeable dress sense, already in my mind I had stripped him down, scrubbed him up and trimmed his beard. As we acknowledged each other, I had potentially removed his long sideburns, then thought, yes, he has potential. After our greetings, we opted for the nearby café situated at the bottom of the park, just behind where we were stood, and he bought me a large coffee. I was nervous, so was chatting the whole time but it seemed George was much quieter and made me feel quite insecure. He didn't put himself out to make me feel overly welcome and it almost felt like he would have preferred me not to have been there at all, but there I was! I remember thinking, I wonder if he would be more impressed with me if I told him I had only just passed my driving test, then I thought to myself, maybe not! He created a very strange atmosphere and I wasn't sure if it was because he was worried about me meeting his elderly mum, or something more than that. We left the park and I went back to my car after he had arranged to meet me outside the park gates in his 4x4 to guide me to his home, where he lived with his mother. I arrived at my car and sat there for a while, wondering if I had made a terrible mistake. I didn't recognise him, he was different to how I had remembered him, so much so that the atmosphere felt cold, almost as if he had a severe hatred for me. At one point I even felt a little frightened of him and shuddered. He pipped his car horn as he drove slowly past and I pulled out from my parking space and steadily drove up behind him. Surprised to see how cautious he drove so as not to lose me amongst the fast-moving traffic and how he waited for me to catch up when I fell too far behind; it was at that point I decided to follow him instead of intention-ally losing him, so I could go straight home. I realised he may not be as bad as all that and thought, maybe I was too quick to jump to conclusions, and began to relax a little.

When we finally reached the bungalow where he and his mother lived I suddenly remembered meeting her before and hoped she would remember me. As I brought my car to a halt in front of their driveway, the first thing I noticed was the beautiful front garden and the array of hanging baskets holding the most impressive display of flowers. I hadn't seen such a display since I visited my father at his flat before he died, and it bought back some lovely memories of him. George was given the privilege of meeting my father when we were young and talking of marriage, so I guess I associated the two and smiled as I climbed out of my car. I walked towards George as he opened the front door to the bungalow and led me inside. I could see by the smoke-tainted walls that there had been heavy smoking going on for some time, and the odour of stale tobacco smoke lingered on the furnishings, adding to the dense smell already in the air. There was a distinct indication of bachelor manifestation and a kind of solitary depression that seemed to hang over the place; tell-tale signs of loneliness and seclusion. Half-empty beer cans had been abandoned and left on the top of the freezer which stood in the large conservatory that housed many foliage plants, some badly in need of watering. The patterned carpet that ran through the whole of the bungalow was a little worse for wear and badly in need of a good clean but nevertheless it seemed George was very proud of their home and invited me to look around. After briefly re-introducing me to his mum he led me through the bungalow to the back garden, where a magnificent array of shrubs and flowers cascade over the sides of the pond and the aroma of night-scented stocks very lightly filled the air. No doubt it was beautiful, and I could see that a lot of time and effort had been spent planning the accuracy of each plant, shrub and flower that had been planted to give it more chance to flourish. There was definitely credit to be given to a man who took such pride in his garden and I believed, as I still do now, that when a man plants a garden he plants seeds of happiness! As I stood gazing over the hedgerows I thought about my old dad and how much he would have loved the views from where I stood. Strange that the memory of him was suddenly triggered as I realised how close George lived to where my dad lived before he died. Remembering the quotation that my dad often recited, I spoke it aloud, "Love what you grow and what you love will grow"... how right he was, and George's garden was proof of that! That afternoon was one of mixed emotions. I wouldn't say that it was the best experience I had ever encountered, as our time together was split between George attending to his mum and kind of working around the fact he hadn't dared to tell her who I was and what I was actually doing there. I got the impression he felt guilty, but I couldn't work out for the life of me why. He hadn't wanted to make it too obvious that I was a female companion and kept me at a distance but, from what I experienced that day, I couldn't get a clear understanding of his role or who was more reliant on whom. I understood that his mum had regular carers to attend to her, but they did not visit during that weekend, as George had postponed them and cancelled her care programme while I was there; and from what I understood it was something he did each time I stayed. After caring many years for his sick father Frank, George's relationship with his mother became strained and I saw nothing but a worn-out man who had given the best years of his life to his forever ageing parents. He had forfeited any claim to happiness that he may have had and struggled with nursing and caring for his parents in-between working as a gardener and developing a twaekondo school. George was not like other men, I knew that, it was something I had learned about him during our first encounter when I was young woman, but I was never quick to judge and always respected honesty. I perhaps knew a lot more about him than his brothers ever did as I don't think they ever really spent time getting to know the person I did. His heart had become hard and his mind over-worked, so much so that he had no time to experience love as it should have been, yet years previously when we initially met he was the most loving, gentle character I had ever known.

I surmised that when he was faced with the devastating trauma of caring for his elderly father, he became so distressed and found the pain of watching him suffer too big a conquest, and after a continuation of severe health problems, it was an absolute shock to him that his father had to have both legs amputated long before he died. George found caring for his father virtually impossible, causing him so much heartache that he lost sight of any future he might have had and denied himself the right to be loved by anyone.

I recall George and I sat in the conservatory chatting all day long, in-between attending to his mother. She could be quite cantankerous and provoked a response in George that up to that point he had kept under control. When he was young, I remembered him being so quiet and placid it would have taken an earthquake to stir him but as a much more mature man he was a lot more irritable. I detected a kind of resentment in his voice as she continually beckoned him to attend to her every whim and it seemed that no matter what he did for her, he never quite got it right and she pulled him over the coals, causing him to react with resentment.

She seemed not to have any recognition of his low spirit or his ageing walk or indeed the difficulties he experienced due to the painful hip he had replaced years prior to that; I was concerned about him but didn't interfere. I noticed he was quite unsteady on his legs and wondered how he had managed to dig over all that earth in the garden and planted and tended to it while continually tending to his very demanding mother. Then he confessed that during the years they had lived together the garden had become his haven of peace where he sought respite after a full day of being opposed, yet also being relied upon. It was difficult to judge a woman who had reached the age of ninety and beyond, but I was almost immediately expected to side with either one or the other – which put me into a very difficult position. What I noticed most about Joan was that her hair had obviously had regular care and hairdressing skills applied, which made the best of her short silver locks. Her features and overall appearance had not changed much since the last time I saw her, all those years ago, apart from her very slightly aged complexion, she was quite beautiful; which I found amazing considering her age. Joan's tiny frame was only slightly smaller than I had remembered, and I immediately warmed to her. I stayed at the bungalow for the whole weekend and spent time reminiscing but when I arrived back home I couldn't get him or his mother out of my head. I felt saddened that I hadn't had the opportunity to meet his father one more time before he died as I felt connected to him by the sad events of our lives. I met Frank all those years before and really liked him, and George said that he liked me too and was pleased we were planning to marry. Occasionally, I would think back to the day

George and I travelled to Surrey to see them and wondered if we had forgotten what was important to us back then; the people who meant the most to us and what a difference to our lives they made? As we recalled our past and remembered all those who were no longer a part of this world I found myself wishing we could have stepped back in time to experience the good times we had with them just one more time. We cried, smiled and empathised with each other as we generally showed sadness as reality hit and we realised there was no going back and that we would always have regrets; we knew that.

George and I arranged to see each other again and over a few months we built up, what I thought was a reasonable relationship with one another. Although there were things to clear up about our previous encounter, we tried to think about the good times, the happy moments and tried not to be haunted by the past. I kept my mind focussed on all the good we had previously experienced and looked towards the future; and all the good that would be following. For a few months our relationship ran quite smoothly, apart from the occasional input from his mother, we had very little to worry about. I helped around the bungalow and got acquainted with Joan as a woman, as opposed to just someone who needed care. I suppose it was natural for her to look on me as one of her carers, but I wanted her to know that I wasn't just a carer! I helped and contributed towards caring for her because I wanted to; not because I had to. It was difficult for her to differentiate between me and the carers but eventually she did refer to me as 'Maree' rather than Rosemarie. The bold, gold cross I wore around my neck helped to differentiate me from the carers and I seemed to gain her trust, and after a while she began to rely on me. I took great care of her while I was there – cut, filed and painted her nails in the colour she liked and ensured she was fed with meals that had all the right nutrients for her frail system when George or the carers weren't there. I took my turn applying cream to her back and legs to prevent her loose skin from drying out and bathed her feet when she suffered with her corns. As time went by I invited George and his mother down to my place, as it seemed I was spending so much time at their bungalow I rarely saw my own family. I missed my grandchildren and pottering around my own home so I thought it would benefit us all if we spent a little time at my place in Market Deeping. George eventually agreed and made arrangements to bring his mum down to see me. I quickly had my broken stairlift repaired so that he could get her up and down stairs to access the bedrooms more easily and I got someone in to help change the furniture around in the spare bedroom to cater for her needs; almost identical to her own room. I must admit she was overjoyed when she arrived at the house, taken aback when she saw how beautiful the conservatory was and how the double doors opened up and gave her immediate access to the garden itself… no need for her to rely on George to manoeuvre her around so she could see the beautiful blue skies and feel the open air on her face. She was mesmerised by it all and asked why I hadn't told her about it before. She went on to say, "I could live here with you, Maree, I'm ninety-two years old, it wouldn't be for long!" I suppose these are the sort of things one feels guilty about when people like Joan pass away. I found it difficult helping to care for her, as her standards had been so high she expected only the best from anyone who took care of her but having certain disabilities myself I had been known to come down with a crunch when I tried too hard and I had to rest up for a while.

I had known George for approximately six months and I still hadn't gotten to know anything about him, he spoke very little about himself, and in fact he spent hours in silence just sat inside the conservatory at the rear of their bungalow, drinking can after can of Stella and white wine that his mother bought in by the case load. I sat alongside him for many hours just trying to encourage conversation, but it seemed he was so full of thoughts and woe he had no desire to speak to me. Sometimes it seemed he was more or less punishing me for wanting to be with him. I tried to analyse his behaviour but when he realised what I was trying to do he became irritable. "Don't try analysing me!" he said. That stopped me in my tracks and I stormed out of the conservatory to go and sit on his bed. It was difficult to get away from stressful situations in such a small bungalow, when his mother occupied the large living room and George the conservatory; it left me with nowhere to go, nowhere to escape to when our discussions became heated. I considered the amount of time he had lived alone as a single man and wondered if I had left it too long to expect anything different from him. He occasionally referred to himself as being a bachelor and I got the impression he liked the thought of that! I also noticed that many of the men who lived near to him were bachelors too; and some of them lived with their mothers just like George did. Where I lived, most of the middle-aged men were married with children and worked locally to support their families, how George had gotten away with remaining single I will never know!

George told me when his father became ill and wanted to live with him his brothers voted George the most appropriate out of the three of them to take care of him; then of course when his father died it was automatically expected for George to take on the role of carer for his mother too. He told me that he had originally moved in with his mother to make it easier for him and company for both of them but became her carer after she had suffered a stroke and was unable to care for herself. Over a period of time I got to realise that the relationship between George and his mother hadn't been an easy one, especially when she began to suffer with confusion and memory loss. I understood only too well how difficult it had been for him throughout the years, as when I stayed at the bungalow I detected the desperation he felt when he couldn't arrange respite. At times he couldn't comply with his mother's requests as he was simply exhausted, which often resulted in her becoming frustrated and losing her temper with him! I sat through episodes of childlike quarrelling and raised voices and at times became concerned for each of them, but then I realised I was becoming part of it all and felt just as frustrated as George.

—⟋⟍—

CHAPTER 12

Tangled Emotions

As advised by my old counsellor, Clive Powell, I still did what I had done for many years and kept a record of situations which occurred while I was recovering from ill health. I had battled long and hard with the effects and trauma of a complete physical breakdown and finally after many years managed to reach what seemingly felt like the final step to recovery. Although agoraphobia was still a problem for me, I struggled hard to get back to what was generally labelled as "the norm" and got tired of fighting off those who were supposed to be supporting me as they had been a hindrance for many years. I no longer had the strength to remain focussed or indeed feel sane around them. Wednesday 8 January 2014 I wrote these notes in a note book I carried around with me… "It has been two long years since I have done any writing. Life has been difficult over the last 5 years, so much has happened I have been reluctant to use my office, as I realise that once I enter into the world of 'Little Molly' I owe it to myself and everyone who has gotten to know me the truth of the final years; as in spite of trying to keep an harmonious relationship with everyone; it seems I have not been able to accomplish that. The word 'vulnerable' automatically springs to mind when I think of myself as 'little Molly' but even as a mature woman I possess certain innocence that seems to attract both 'the undesirable' and 'oppressive' individuals who burden me with their angry, oppositional and argumentative forces. Blinded by my need to be loved I have associated myself with those who have found it easy to use and abuse me. It seemed to be that my own worst enemy has become my autobiography, *Little Molly*...."

I had often wondered if it was a good idea to write about my abusive childhood and even after thinking about it long and hard before I made the decision, I still had doubts about it. I expected a certain amount of conflict and disapproval from obvious members of my family but never expected to experience so much disapproval from those I held so dear. Although I expected everyone to have their own personal opinion about the book, I couldn't digest the fact that certain family members seemed outraged by the fact I had cast shame amongst the family; after all the years they had managed to keep the child abuse amongst our family concealed. Some members of my family even publicly announced their disbelief of the possibility a grown man could commit such indecencies to a child as young as four; although they are obviously aware of the news headlines and reporters who have the unbearable job of announcing incidents of child abduction, rape and indecent assaults on young children, even today! I have learned many things about my family and about life itself since I wrote, *Little Molly*. I have listened to opinions and thoughts on child abuse and although I would say that the majority of people I know are against child abuse, there are the small minority who would prefer to verbally and mentally attack a victim, as opposed to reprimanding a paedophile or an abuser! I learned many years ago, when I was a child growing up, that some close family members had problems accepting that at four years of age I could not fight off an abuser who was ten years my senior; or control the amount of abuse I suffered. But when I began to write, *Little Molly* I never really gave any thought to the devastation I might bestow on myself as a result of writing it! Since *Little Molly* was first published, certain family members have caused me so much grief, anxiety and, above all, made every effort to destroy my reputation for being honest and open regarding the terrible inflictions I incurred as a child. During the last ten years I have experienced the pain and repercussions child abuse has had on my life, particularly as a younger member of a very large family. Writing *Little Molly* has caused many to hate me; supposedly close, caring members of my family have suddenly amalgamated with friends and associates and turned against me; they have become hateful enemies! I have very often wondered what their opinion of child abuse would be if they were publicly put on the spot and asked to give their opinion for everyone to hear, would they so readily protect the paedophiles and offer them lodgings to live amongst their own children? I suspect they would! I've asked myself this question over and over again and wonder, is it because they merely do not understand the seriousness of child abuse, or is it because they simply don't care? Then I think about all the children who have been sexually and physically abused, many who have not lived to tell their story, my stomach churns as I feel physically sickened by it all; this gives me more understanding of why acts of sexual abuse towards children is so damn difficult to stop! I can now understand why so many abuse cases never make it into the court room! My advice to parents and grandparents is, take on board what I have written in both *Little Molly* and *Molly II (Am I Who I Should Be?)* as I consider it is every parent's duty to understand about child abuse and how high the percentage is of children abused within their own homes – listen to the child and take note of all those who have experienced it – doubting their word will not make it non-existent! Only then will they help towards protecting generations of children. I have experienced nothing but repugnance from some of the closest members of my family who I thought would have understood, but like so many they have not been educated about the effects of child abuse, or how to prevent it; only when we are educated in recognising an abuser will our children be safe! Although I have wondered if writing, *Little Molly* was worth the amount of pain and anguish it caused me, I think back to the crippling mental state I was in before my counsellor Clive Powell taught me how to unload all the terrifying experiences into my journals; then I realise how necessary it was. At the age of fifty-seven I realise just how much time I have spent on my own, crying and feeling unworthy; wondering how on earth I could continue to love when so many have done me harm. Despite my inability to forget the abuse I have suffered, I have tried to put it to rest, but the power of remembering is forceful and drives a wedge between everyone I love. Like a repellent, it poisons the air and brings out the worst in everyone. Although at times I have, as an unsuspecting victim, felt myself being reeled in to situations that could have proven to be disastrous, I did not; and neither was I willing to enter into such disrepute! I have regularly questioned my role as a mother and my capability to cause such an imprint on the mind of an offspring, as I have been accused of causing others to react to situations violently, but I want all those who once judged me for being "a victim" to know I was not to blame for the abuse I suffered and neither am I accountable for resemblances related by descent. My abuser, John Wass, was born to my mother a decade before I was… I take no responsibility for that or for his actions! I have lived a whole lifetime trying to make amends for mistake that my brother John Wass made, admittedly I made a few of my own along the way but I wasn't convinced I had made as many mistakes as some people would have liked me to believe and indeed make me accountable for, but I have cowered and accepted fault to earn respect from family members and the few people I entertained. But then somewhere in the midst of writing *Little Molly* and researching my background, I came to terms with my family's history and realised they were blaming the wrong person! I was the victim – not the abuser! It seemed I had become a target… everyone I once trusted and believed in either criticised, blamed, slandered or verbally abused me. I overheard conversations relating to me and my private affairs, my appearance and the way I dressed was frowned upon by those who could have, but didn't, take time to meet my standards. My forever draining confidence was susceptible to unkind remarks, hence disagreeable situations occurred and my health was drastically affected by it all; the price I had to pay for not having the strength to counteract what they conspired.

While I morbidly moved from room to room in the house I had lived in for almost twenty years, I no longer referred to it as being my home. I was sad and felt very lonely, although my youngest sibling lived only three doors away we had become estranged and I felt trapped by circumstance. It took me a few years to accept I had, once again, become a victim of a different type of abuse. Living in the middle of a council estate I suffered a degree of exploitation and slander as my name was put up all over Facebook and other multimedia groups. I could only suppose that was done in order to defame and injure my character; hoping it would interfere with my becoming a successful writer and author. After I had struggled to write and publish *Little Molly* the attacks of slander, insults and false reports became more apparent to me, as those responsible cast reflections on my character by making damaging implications by discrediting me in public, behind my back, and cast aspersions when they wrote on Facebook that, "Any normal person could have written *Little Molly*; and with little effort." I was devastated when I was first told about the messages publicised on Facebook and could not comprehend why anyone would want to do that. At first, I thought, possibly a reaction to reading it, which I might have been able to understand, but when I was informed the person had not read it and the slander became worse and prolonged, I knew it was for no other reasons but thoughtlessness and malice.

When I think about the terrible hardship I have had to face since I left the Derbyshire care system as a child, I have never really had the courage to face the world full on, by that I mean I still cocoon myself inside the shell I crawled into when I was just a small child, and what made it worse was the fact that no one really knew what had happened to cause such a reaction. For all the psychologists, psychiatrists and specialists I have met since I left the care homes, none have been able to fully understand what life was like for me after 'parental separation' and the challenges I faced once I had reached my teenage years; because no one understood it, they labelled it "rebeldom".... But this was not the case at all!

I personally believe that children who are removed from their parents, for whatever reason, are kind of shell shocked. Thinking back to my own experiences, after a traumatic period of abuse, neglect and family breakup and, let's call it, "misunderstandings" of both the authorities and my parents, I became quiet and withdrew from situations I was frightened of. I didn't understand why I was suffering such devastating feelings, like I was mourning for loved ones who I had lost, losing the only security I knew became fixed inside my mind and at that particular time that's really all I could think about. But as time progressed, my mind focussed solely on survival and I picked up everything that was said regarding my parents, what they were being accused of and what might happen inside the court room the day we were all to attend court; that day was logged inside my brain and remained there throughout my entire life.

The moment my younger siblings and I were removed from our parents' home and placed with strangers, we tried to survive inside various children's homes which were alien to us. We were given a completely new set of rules and regulations and moulded into totally different people from who we were. The years passed by and when the time came we were re-introduced to our biological parents, that's where we experienced even greater difficulties! They themselves had suffered many problems trying to arrange visits to see us, but we had been placed so far out in the Peak District, a rural area where there was very little transport available, so on the rare occasions they did get to see us they no longer knew us!

Since the human race became civilized we have been able to make choices and do what is considered to be "the right thing" so it seems only natural for parents to receive children back into their lives once they have grown, but then parents often become a target; someone the child presumes is to blame for their misfortune! What happens next depends on each individual and how capable they are of handling the situation.

In mine and my youngest daughter's case, because of the length of time she was away from me and the condition of my health, we both experienced many problems, which resulted in my mental health remaining poor and hers being affected too. In many ways her life mirrored mine, but I hoped she realised it was neither my nor her fault; it was never what I wanted for her or her siblings. I have always loved them and shall love them till the day I die. I ask for nothing from my children, only that they will try to understand more about my childhood and the way I was raised; in that way they will understand more about their own lives and the way they were raised! I would like to think that I have managed to pass on to them lots of knowledge and skills but most of all the ability to empathise when the need arises; things that do not come naturally to us!

Saturday 25 July 2015, I struggled to remain focussed on what I had planned to be the final manuscript of my autobiography. Thinking back to the conversation I once had with my eldest daughter Cheniel, when she expressed her thoughts about the book and her sudden realisation that I had not experienced what society would refer to as a "normal upbringing". She expressed her sadness regarding the fact I had written so many sad things about her grandmother; and at that time, I found it difficult to explain to her how much my mother (her grandmother) had changed over the years. Once my mother had become independent and more successful, despite the many years of hardship and difficulty she had as a young mother, she had become a pillar of society and attended church regularly. Throughout many years she worked as a carer for Nottinghamshire County Council, caring for the elderly, and told me often that she loved her work. She was a strong, hearty woman and travelled to work on a moped through thick snow blizzards, rain or shine to attend to people who needed her; knowing there would be many staff members who didn't turn up for work. Prior to that, she struggled, paying landladies for lodgings where she lived, and by the time Cheniel was born she had obtained a mortgage and bought her own house, while contributing towards many different charities, as well as paying a contribution of maintenance to Derbyshire Social Services Department for me and my younger siblings, when years after the fact, she was billed for the care we received and almost went to prison for overlooking it! She tried to make amends for all the heartache we had suffered, and despite her faults, no matter what happened, when we reached adulthood she was always there for us. She had made mistakes and she knew that, but the truth was she really didn't get the support she needed. She had given birth to a family of strong, independent individuals, each counteracting whatever decisions she made; she was no match for my brother, John Wass, or indeed many of us. She taught us many things and despite the fact we didn't always listen to what she had to say, I for one have never forgotten what she worked all her life for.... To leave us, her children, as comfortable as she could – and didn't forget to add in her last will and testament that she always loved us; that meant more to me than anything!

I think we forget how much she did for us when we were raising our own children and hit hard times. By the time Cheniel was old enough to attend school my mother had made her way in the world and was respected by many people. Considering the hard life and desperate choices she had to make as a young mother, I considered her to be a legend. Life had been tough on her, and even I did not know everything about her, it was only when I first spoke to my cousin Norman on Facebook a few years ago that I realised, I never really knew her at all; and if the truth is to be known I doubt if any of us ever did! Mother always maintained that she never abandoned us in the family home at Eckington, but she did have trouble trying to feed and control us all and because of that she was victimised by the people who lived around us. She told me that she left my sister Anne in charge but I think she failed to understand that Anne worked away from home and could not stay home with us, as she would have lost her job. Anne did the best she could, I can vouch for that, but it just wasn't enough. Mother told me she had suffered with her nerves since the day she moved away from her own mother, who gave her loads of support when she was alive. And that she had her first nervous breakdown after giving birth to my older brother, David, when she moved from Mosborough to Eckington, despite the fact they were just a few miles apart she felt isolated in the small mining community where she didn't know anyone. She struggled for a lot of years before she finally reached the point where she felt unable to cope and appeared on ITV's *The Friday Night Programme* that came on television at 6pm, when she put several of her children up for adoption; I'm not sure if I was born then! She was ridiculed for that, and again when she asked for help in a local newspaper; desperate measures were taken well before she finally left us. I surmise it was at this point she felt she had no choice but to leave us with our older siblings, until such time as she had found another place for us all to live and a better paying job, but by the time she had built up another home it was far too late. When I was removed from the care homes and placed with my mother at the age of fourteen, she literally begged me to write a book so the truth could be told. She repeatedly told me about the struggles she experienced and the kind of things that seemed to go against everything she did for us, but I had lots of problems at that time and my life was so chaotic I never thought I would ever get to think straight again. My older siblings told me different version of what had happened before Mother left and I honestly thought they had forgotten I was there too; I remembered most things! It was never my intentions to write these books in the context that they have been written as I really wanted to believe that the bad stuff hadn't happened, but then I figured if I was brave enough to write about my life in the first place, then I was brave enough to write the truth! It was always difficult for me to accept that I had been abandoned as a child and I guess many of us would not have classed it as such, as there were older brothers and sisters coming and going who were more than capable of taking care of me and my younger siblings, but of course they were children too and in the eyes of the law were not responsible. I never doubted my mother's word regarding the incidents that lead up to her leaving us, as I do still remember her being accused of missing payments of rent for the tenancy she was given to raise her family in 4, Beech Crescent, Eckington, near Sheffield. When I was fourteen I studied the rent book which she kept till her dying day that showed that she had made regular payments of rent until the day she moved out... Something had gone wrong and she couldn't put it right. For whatever reason, my father left her to fend for herself as well as her family and somewhere along the line things did not work out and she was judged by each and every one of us!

When I gave birth to my own children, Mother contributed towards buying their toys, Ian's first bicycle and his ride-on tractors, Cheniel's roller boots and even some of the twin's shoes, but I also recall her buying coats and clothes for the less fortunate of her grandchildren, things their parents would never have been able to afford had it not been for her. It was inevitable that by the time our children were old enough to make judgements they judged their grandmother fairly when they referred to her as being a "lovely grandmother" and I see clearly why they loved her so much. Throughout the many years of raising my own children, I invited my mother to all our Christmas activities, parties and trips out. She spent a considerable amount of time with us and as a result of that, my children loved her, just as I did. There is so much more I could write about my mother, the happy moments I experienced with her and the laughter we shared but it proves too much for me and I feel that my heart just would not stand it, so before I lay her to rest I would just like to take a moment to tell her how much I really loved her and to say, "I did it, Mam! I wrote those books, but it was my story; the way I remembered it!"

᎒Ꮟ CHAPTER 13 Ꮟ᎒

Equal Priority

I haven't spent much time in my office over the last year or so, anything I have added to, *Molly III* has been written in note pads and journals that I scattered around my desk while I was thinking about other people instead of my own life and where it was going! My life has been a shambles, really, so full of putting every effort into making other people happy; I have failed yet again to put my own needs as an equal priority. I always got the impression that people thought my life was far less important than theirs and so I wonder, was it something I did wrong... is it because I am a far less a person than others or have I come to naturally accept being treated differently? Someone I once held close to my heart recommended that I should toughen up, but my answer to him was always the same, "Why should I change my personality and my caring persona just to protect myself from those who make a habit of using me?" When I was a young woman my mother always told me, 'You think with your heart, not your brain' – I fear she was right!

Every time I faced a situation within a relationship, it reached the point when I asked myself, should I stay? Knowing I was going to be the broken loser who gave far more than I should have done or leave to protect the little bit of dignity I was left with? Although my mind was always set on running away from problems, there were times when the love in my heart anchored me; like a ship on the shore. I fear I fall in love too quickly and feel too deeply for my own good!

I recall the evening of 19 December 2014. My relationships with the closest people to me seemed to be failing and I developed a strong suspicion that several of those I once trusted were conspiring against me. I had been feeling uneasy around my ex-partner, who I had lived apart from for almost five years, but when we agreed to separate he moved just around the corner from me and began associating with a young woman called Kitty who he had gotten to know years previously, when he asked me to help her through a custody battle against the social services. Despite my ill health I agreed and spent two whole years trying to battle with solicitors, barristers and the local authority on her behalf. She was a nineteen-year-old girl with special needs! That seemed to be one of the facts that was hurled at me when I first met her and over a period of time I picked up on things about her and her family that I wouldn't have, had the nature of our childhoods not been so similar. It was because of that I recognised the devastating effects that, in my opinion, had been caused by severe child abuse… we were similar in some respects and yet so far apart in others! I was originally introduced to her by her mother, Maureen, who had also been placed into a category of women labelled by social services as "hard of learning". I had been told by my friend Lola that over a period of many years they had been subject to ridicule and name-calling in and around our community, until I took the family under my wing. Both mother and daughter suffered to the extent that they were too frightened to walk the streets at night, particularly during Halloween, when many of the locals found it necessary to hurl eggs and flour at the windows and door of the family's home which was situated on the corner of Wellington Way in Market Deeping. Fortunately, by that time, they had gotten to know me, and I was able to calm Kitty down each time she suffered a hysterical attack, which the crisis team couldn't achieve without sedation. Suffering from learning difficulties it was virtually impossible for Maureen and her family to reason with the assailants or in fact explain to anyone what was happening to them. The police responded to several 999 calls, but soon after they left Maureen's home it would happen all over again. That sort of thing happened at Halloween and although it seemed quite innocent and childlike I wasn't about to stand by and let it happen to a family who couldn't really cope with it. It took months to settle Kitty down and although Maureen and I spoke with the police and medical experts about the way it affected her health, they said there was little they could do, so the family applied to the South Kesteven District Council who granted them a mutual exchange of their property for one in a different area. At first, they went to live in Bourne, a small town just outside Market Deeping but it seemed the trouble followed them and before we knew it they had been transferred into a bungalow on Milfield Road, the other side of Market Deeping. It was a lovely area and they seemed to settle in quite well and quickly put the past behind them. In no time at all, Kitty had decorated her bedroom with Liverpool football team memorabilia and often visited mine and Peter Senior's home with her mother Maureen just to tell us what she had bought new. Occasionally, she ran little errands and helped around the house, I was slowly recovering from a complete physical breakdown, so appreciated her and Maureen's help. It must have been at least a year before Kitty told us that she had met a young man who lived quite close to the family and within no time at all she announced that she was pregnant. She hadn't been educated regarding the possibilities of her becoming pregnant, or in fact contraception. Having spent many years in foster care she was looked upon as a child; even when she left the care homes and reached the age of twenty-two her family still perceived her as being a child, but I had studied Kitty long and hard and realised she was not the child they thought and was far more aware than anyone gave her credit for. While spending time with her I realised how much she wanted them to accept her as a "normal adult", she wanted to be like you and me. Being the same age as my youngest children, Kyle and Allishia, it gave me something to work on, a guide to go by, so my work began! I had already gotten to know her quite well, having spent time with her and her mum I had noticed that even her mum took advantage of her inability to count and recognise the value of our currency. Kitty needed to learn that a handful of pennies amounting to £3 were far less than the handful of £20 notes that she loosely held in her hand, but her mum was happy for her daughter to believe they were worthless and quickly gathered the notes to put them into her own purse when Kitty referred to them as being "paper" rubbish for the bin! As much as I liked Maureen I could not stand by and let that happen, the only thing that seemed important to Maureen was the easy lifestyle she had become accustomed to, despite having special needs herself she was totally aware that no one would ever be concerned about Kitty's life and no one would question the amount of money she was taking from her. They had both been dragged through the care system and cast aside to fend for themselves when they reached eighteen. They attended a special needs school but as far as I know, Maureen wasn't a boarder but was still left to fend for herself as soon as the social services department considered her of age. In a society that took people like her for granted, she learned to fend for herself and took care of her family the best way she knew how. Manipulating Kitty into handing over the majority of her Disablement Allowance was just another survival tactic; one that did not benefit Kitty! After witnessing Maureen manipulating Kitty into handing over the majority of the benefit she received each fortnight, I decided it was time to teach Kitty the value of money and how to read and write. It was at that point I realised how well I had come through the trauma caused by severe child abuse and although I tried not to compare my own childhood abuse with Kitty's, it was obvious to me that the devastation had caused similar difficulties in us both – reading, writing and arithmetic were something we had no or very little knowledge of; every subject that took a clear mind to achieve we struggled with.

When Kitty was three months pregnant I began to work with her, I thought if I could just teach her a little of what I had learned, it would prove to me that she was able to remember, learn and improve. Although I had difficulties at school, I came out with a little knowledge but a lot of common sense and something told me that Kitty just hadn't been given a chance. I hoped what I had learned was enough to teach Kitty a few simple basics, although it seemed all the odds were against me, I remembered what I had been taught in class; with a little perseverance I could achieve anything – this was not only a test for Kitty but also a test for me too! When I first suggested it to Kitty she seemed uninterested, like she had no use for it at all but after explaining to her in simple terms how important it was for her to learn now that she was having a baby, the penny seemed to drop, and she was far more eager to start learning. I hadn't a clue how I was going to teach her, and I must admit the thought of her attending a special needs school and leaving without any knowledge of the simplest of maths, I wondered if I was just kidding myself. Then I thought back to my own school days and lack of achievements and how much I had learned since leaving school, so I threw caution to the wind and went headlong into teaching mode, I had to give it a go – if only for the benefit of her unborn baby. I worked with Kitty on and off throughout her pregnancy and continued even after the birth of her baby girl, Elle. Within time I noticed a big change in Kitty's understanding of our currency and the way she spoke; having noticed that she had a severe speech impediment, I naturally fell into the routine of giving her elocution lessons, simply because no one was able to understand the confusion of noises she uttered. She mumbled in a broken, jumbled up English kind of way, like a toddler who had never been taught to speak properly and I was convinced that she had been really neglected. Having spent years of her childhood being raised within Lincolnshire foster homes it seemed she had never been given the correct help and support that was required to manipulate her brain into functioning properly. I believed that everyone who was involved with Kitty accepted her inability to speak and put it down to her disabilities, but I wanted to challenge that! For someone who exhibited learning difficulties, she had a terrific memory and I quickly picked up on things like the lists of dates for appointments that she never wrote down but recalled several months later. She could recite everything I had said, word for word and reel off every name of the Liverpool football team managers and even extended her awareness of other team's players too. I wondered many times if she had a photographic memory, but I never got to know that! I began teaching her to write her name and simple words like cat, rat, mat, and each day I added another few words and asked her to pronounce each one. I deliberately exaggerated each word I spoke and slipped in a nursery rhyme just to make it fun. I purchased pens, paper, crayons and lots of activity products to help her with her co-ordination skills, as she had difficulty manoeuvring and guiding objects around certain obstacles. I got her to regularly count currency until she perfected it and was able to purchase items from the shops by herself and knew when she had been short changed! I showed her how to sterilise her baby equipment and how to make up bottle feeds, although my daughter Allishia could take credit for that too! By the time I had finished she was speaking much more clearly, but I did notice that each time she mixed with members of her own family she lost much of her ability to pronounce certain words and struggled to string sentences together and seemed to revert back to how it was when I first met her; and so, the elocution lessons began again. I believe Kitty was offered very little, if any at all, specialised medical care or supportive care to assist in her rehabilitation after being sexually abused as a child, as far as she recalls she received no long-term counselling or psychiatric help while being under the care of Lincolnshire Social Services Department. Naturally this affected her, but she never allowed it to interfere with her love and care for her baby Elle. Lincolnshire Social Services categorised Elle well before Kitty gave birth to her, solely because of Maureen's inappropriate care of Kitty and her siblings when they were small, but no one took into account how Kitty had been let down by the social services department and "the system" while being in their care! The NCH (Leaving Care Team) signed Kitty out of their care when she was only nineteen, satisfied that she was capable of working and making a life for herself. When she took over her own life and tried the best she could, she was penalised for it! No one gave her credit for anything that she did and despite her achievement to pass a full year's care assessment for her ability to care for her own baby, she lost her anyway. Elle was taken from Kitty by Lincolnshire Social Services Department during the last few weeks of the assessment, having failed for allowing an undesirable to visit the county-run assessment centre where her social worker had transferred her to. That centre had staff on duty 24\7 and could have prevented anyone entering the security doors that enabled them access to Kitty's room, but they failed to do that too!

Kitty achieved many things when she was a child, her Intermediate, Bronze, Silver, Gold and Life-Savers Certificates which are just a few to mention, but I failed to see any positive report submitted on her behalf when she appeared in the Lincolnshire High Court fighting for custody of her own baby. It seemed that Kitty and her baby, amongst many more, including myself have suffered the aftermath of being an "abused child" and a "child in care" despite initially being labelled "The Innocent Child", it was "The Innocent Child" who eventually paid a heavy price!

—m—

CHAPTER 14

Friends Or Foes

When Peter Senior and I separated, I desperately tried to move on with my life, but it seemed impossible, as I came face-to-face with some very worrying circumstances and although I constantly tried to ignore situations that arose, I found myself deep in battle with the ones who revolved around my life and looked for weaknesses and insecurities in me. Since suffering the nervous breakdown I had never been able to build my life up to the standard it was before, not only because of people draining me of my finances but also working alongside each other to make me doubt my own capabilities, thoughts and judgements. I found myself in a situation where I was advised to move out of my own home, where I had lived for twenty years, just to guarantee my own safety. I was reluctant to be scared off by people who enjoyed playing psychological games with me, although there seemed to be little or no laws in this country to protect vulnerable people who have suffered mental health problems I was reluctant to be chased away by those who hounded me. I had so much to be afraid of, but I was determined not to give in to those who were a part of it. It was very difficult for me to determine who I could trust and who I could not and

even the closest individuals had been subject to my suspicions, and although I would have preferred to think
I could have trusted George, I was often plagued with
coincidental circumstances that led me to believe otherwise. For many years I had wondered about Peter
Senior's loyalty to me and my family and at one stage I
felt sure he had betrayed both me and my children. I can
only go on his behaviour towards me since our breakup
and of course the actions I felt he had taken to turn my
own family against me while he remained in their
favour. I feel at this point I have to be careful not to
write anything that may provoke the response I had
from some of them last Christmas, when George, Peter,
Kitty and several of their friends became very hostile
and avoided me to the extent where, even though they
spent the run up of the Christmas holidays in the same
vicinity as my home, I hardly saw them! I have to admit
I became a total wreck overnight, when it seemed to me
that they fuelled each other's morale and Peter Senior's
care for me was negligible despite him receiving almost
six hundred pounds per month for care duties. On the
evening of 19 December 2014, each one of them became
elusive and despite insisting they were not in contact
with each other, all their mobile phones rejected my
calls and it seemed whatever vicinity George was in,
Peter, Kitty and her sister was there too. As a result of
spending almost two years helping George and trying to
make things easier for him and his mother, I spent the
run up to Christmas on my own, phoning first George
and then Peter, just listening to their voicemails saying,
"the person you are calling cannot take your call right
now". I cried most of the season and got into a right
state through it all, the worst feeling of rejection I had

felt since my parents had abandoned me as a child. I surmised this small group of individuals had amalgamated and were toying with me and my emotions and when I sat and thought about what was happening around me, I realised I was being pushed to my limits and felt that Peter Senior was manipulating his friends into frequently and systematically withholding factual information and replacing it with false information; causing me total confusion and torment. I couldn't work out why any of them would want to do this to me or whether they would benefit from it; I just knew they were doing it!

After years of worrying and crying I tried to work things out on my own, the word 'gaslighting' was mentioned by someone I confided in, but the word meant absolutely nothing to me. Then I typed into my computer the key words of all the abusive symptoms I was suffering, and then a whole lot of information came up on my screen and fitted it perfectly. I read a whole lot of stuff that night and was shocked to find that the description it gave for 'gaslighting' was exactly the nature of abuse I was suffering; up until that point I hadn't realised that there was such a word to fit my ordeals. To my astonishment, Google delivered a whole lot of information and although I had been told by many that Google was not the best place to look, it informed me that gaslighting was a form of psychological abuse used by narcissists in order to instil an extreme sense of anxiety and confusion into their victims, to the point where they no longer trust their own memory, perception or judgement; exactly how they made me feel!

"The techniques used in 'gaslighting' are similar to those used in brainwashing, interrogation and torture.

The intention is to, in a systematic way, target the victim's mental equilibrium, self-confidence and self-esteem so that they are no longer able to function in an independent way. It involves the abuser frequently and systematically withholding factual information from the victim and replacing it with false information. Because of its subtlety, this cunning Machiavellian behaviour is a deeply insidious set of manipulations that is difficult for anyone to work out, and with time it finally undermines the mental stability of the victim. The emotional damage is huge when a victim is exposed to it for long enough, they begin to lose their sense of their own self with the inability to trust their own judgements; they start to question the reality of everything in their life, second-guessing themselves and this makes them become very insecure around their own decision-making, even around the smallest of choices. The victim becomes depressed and withdrawn; totally dependent on the abuser for their sense of reality. It is deliberate and progressive in nature, between one individual (the gaslighter) and another (the gaslightee). The Gaslighting effect involves an insidious set of psychological manipulations that are carried out gradually in stages and repeated time after time in order to undermine the mental stability of its victim. It is truly a convoluted dance, where finally the unsuspecting victim believes they are going crazy. Anyone can become the victim of these Gaslighting manoeuvres; age, intelligence, gender, creed is no barrier against narcissistic abuse of this kind. It does not only apply in romantic relationships, it can occur in all different types of relationships; between parent and child, siblings, friends and work colleague, Actually, it can happen between any two people in any walk of life if the intention is there. As a harassment technique it starts with a serious of subtle mind games that intentionally prey on the victims' limited ability to tolerate ambiguity or uncertainty. This is done in order to undercut the victims trust in their own sense of reality, thus resulting in confusion and perplexity for the victim. Even when the victim is bewildered and left wondering, what just happened there, there is a reluctance to see the abuser for what they really are, and it is this denial that is the cornerstone of the Gaslighting relationship. Such abusers manipulate their victims for personal gain, with precision they are able to "pull the strings" of their victims without detection; and render them helpless. In order to understand how a person becomes "a victim" in the first place, it is important to know that the abuser has many faces (the proverbial man or woman for all seasons).

This type of abuse does not happen all at once, it happens in stages which means that if the victim suspects (in early stages) that they are being targeted, they can protect themselves by walking away (physically and metaphorically). However, one needs to be educated and informed as to what signs to look for, this will help victims to understand and identify what is happening at different stages in any interpersonal-relationship (whether at home, work or socially); and guard themselves by keeping the abuser out of their energy field. At the beginning of an abusive relationship the abuser showers the victim with attention, they are loving, charming and flirtatious; and great fun to be with. They appear to be happy and interested in the relationship and the unsuspecting victim enjoys every moment with their new charismatic partner. They love how they get drunk on life, so they too want to drink the elixir with them. Intense bonding begins for the victim, and innocently, they believe their partner feels the same way about them; that the relationship is reciprocal, but this is a narcissist's biggest deception and the victim becomes "hooked"!

Victims are known to experience biochemical changes in the body and structural changes in the brain. These exciting hooks create a release of chemicals (endorphins) in the brain, and it is these endorphins (or pleasure substances) that make the victim feel the euphoria in the first phase of the relationship; like an addict, the victim becomes addicted to the highs; and their suitor too! Having determined the victim's strengths and weaknesses the abuser turns cold, unfeeling, and bitingly cruel, and the victim's fall from grace is a hard one; as if they can do nothing right anymore. They find themselves devalued at every turn, totally confused, they become increasingly stressed, unhappy and depressed with the situation. The rollercoaster relationship leaves a victim in a state of constant chaos, as if always "walking on eggshells". Every ounce of energy they have is directed at defending themselves and working harder and harder to please their abuser in the hopes of getting the relationship back to where it was in the start; when it felt safe. Deprived, the victim is suddenly thrown into strong withdrawal symptoms. They are distraught with anxiety, turned inside out with confusion, and bereft of what they thought they had; a soul-mate. In order to cope with the pain of this deep wound of abandonment and rejection, they escape into a range of unconscious defence mechanisms (a mix of denial, rationalisation, infantile regressive patterns, cognitive dissonance, trauma bonding etc.) alone and isolated from the real world, these behaviours become their only way of surviving the abuse they are now experiencing. The victim becomes the hostage that is overly dependent on their abuser where they are reduced to a shadow of their former self at the mercy of the whims and pleasures of their abuser. The more the victim shows their distress the more important and powerful the abuser gets to feel, hence the more blatant their verbal and physical violence becomes. This "pull, shove" scenario leaves the abuser acting in a way that says, "I hate you, but don't you dare leave me". Therefore, any show of self-determination by the victim will be devalued. Devaluation of the victim can be delivered through many different forms and levels of attack; through victim's own attachment needs, their intellectual capabilities, physical body, sexuality, creativity etc. By this time the victim has been conditioned and appears to the outside world that they are willing partners and even if they do manage to escape from that individual, they are at high risk of future re-victimisation and entrapment with others; because they are primed in a way that other abusers can spot.

Victims are left confused and raw with emotion, eager to find solutions in order to "fix" the dying relationship. However, the abuser resists all attempts to rescue the relationship and will bully with silence or if there is any kind of response, it will be brutally cold. In effect, the victim has become "worthlessly inferior" to them; they know they have drained the victim dry and move on to the next source of supply. Any undertaking to win the abuser back will only feed the abusers ego and provide them with a transient source of narcissistic supply.

Victims find themselves going through emotional and psychological states of mind; disbelief, defence and depression. It is an extreme form of emotional abuse to manipulate the innocent victim. The effects are so insidious, that they can lead to the victim losing all trust in their own judgement and reality. The victim's initial reaction to the abusive behaviour is one of utter disbelief; they cannot believe the sudden change towards them, or indeed the fact that they have been targeted in the first place. All they know is that something terribly odd seems to be happening, but they cannot figure out exactly what it is. Of course, this is precisely what the abuser wants; after all, it would not work if the victim knew what was happening. The method used by the abuser in the initial stage of the relationship progresses in such a way that it virtually guarantees that the victim will become hooked utterly and completely to their abuser. Blinded by their love, the victim naturally trusts and holds the abuser in "good heart", while they become highly critical of them. The sympathy and support that had once been available has now turned to distain and antagonism. Whenever the victim wants to reasonably discuss what is happening in the relationship, they are met with silence, or worse, they find that everything that is being said is twisted or trivialized.

This type of abuse does not have to be severe to have severe consequences on the victim; it can be as subtle as being told that, "you are so sensitive", or that they should not do something because, "you are not able to do it, leave it to me". Even though the victim can rationalise that these statements are untrue, gradually their confidence is being eroded away to such an extent they cannot trust themselves. The abuser has typical traits such as moving items from place to place and then denying that they had moved them at all creating huge confusion to the victim. Or saying something, and then later denying that they had said such a thing. All of this has the psychological effect of making the victim doubt their own memory or perception of events. Desperate for the abuser's approval and reassurance that they are not going mad, the victim becomes very dependent on their abuser; for a sense of reality.

At this stage the victim still has enough of their self to fight and defend themselves against the abuser's manipulation. However, it is beginning to do what it intended to do, that is, to throw the victim off balance by creating self-doubt, angst, turmoil, and guilt. This emotional damage causes the victim, over time, to lose their sense of reality, and sense of self. Becoming lost, confused and unable to trust their own instincts and memory, they tend to isolate themselves because of the shame they feel. Before long, their psychic energy becomes depleted, and they are left unable to defend themselves from the horrendous effect. At this stage the victim feels that they are in danger of being utterly destroyed, they barely recognise themselves and are quickly becoming a shadow of their own self. Living under tyranny they are controlled physically and emotionally, unable to make decisions they are stripped of dignity and safety; they exist in a joyless life and escape into depression. Many victims go on to experience Post-Traumatic Stress Disorder (PTSD) the diagnoses of PTSD can be made based on certain symptoms being present, and these symptoms fall into three categories:

1. *Reliving: (Flashbacks, intrusive imagery, nightmares, anxiety etc.)*
2. *Avoidance: (Avoiding people, places or thoughts, emotional hopelessness etc.)*
3. *Arousal: (Difficulty concentrating, irritability, outbursts of anger, insomnia, hyper-vigilance etc.)" *

Upon reading this I realised what they were doing to me and that it had actually got a name; and to be honest I couldn't think of anything I was able to do to counteract the damage they caused me. I had no trust in any of them and realised for my own sake and safety I had to remain strong and do what I thought was right. Rightly so, I was shocked but what happened last year during the run up to Christmas and over the New Year I began to understand what Peter Senior, George and their friends had tried to achieve. I was not in denial or in disbelief but profoundly sad; I wondered how they had managed to trick me and build up such an array of torturous events and almost succeeded in convincing even the cleverest of people that I was going crazy. They had not only exploited me but others too, for them I felt sorrier as they only had the mental capacity of a child and have no chance of surviving it, help is just around the corner, but who's going to point them into the right direction? I guess I was one of the lucky ones, or I hope to be, as only last week, Wednesday 12 August 2015, I was brave enough to open up to a member of the staff at The Resource Centre in Stamford and told her what I had been going through. Despite the fact that she was

---

* www.psychologytoday.com

trained in this field I still found it very difficult to express all my concerns for fear of what has now become the obvious; that I couldn't prove I was sane! Although I had previously spoken to my own GP, Dr Wilson, several psychiatrists, psychologists, friends and certain family members, I realised what I had become to them, but no one seemed to truly appreciate or understand the deep suffering I was going through. The fact I survived the torturous effects was truly a miracle and a magnificent show of strength, but my confidence had been eroded by the constant battle between me and them. I lived in constant fear of doing the wrong thing and making my situation worse, I worried about, how it could all turn out and felt humiliated when I was told I was a "Drama Queen". Although I tried to ignore all the shameful glances and remarks from those who lived in my community, I suspected they knew absolutely nothing of "narcissistic abuse" so could only believe what they were told by the abuser's themselves. Originally, I thought this group was creating all kinds of situations to try and force me out of my home, as I had been told so many times that I should move out because I live alone, but after twenty long years of living in the same house it wasn't as simple as that. I had been made aware that many young families all over the country wanted to be re-housed into new homes instead of living in flats, but I just wasn't ready to give up my home, and without anyone to help me with my affairs, I had very little chance of finding myself a more suitable accommodation away from here!

—◊◊◊—

CHAPTER 15

Enough Is Enough!

I had struggled all of my life, trying to survive in a world that seemingly was against those who had been raised in such an unfortunate manner as me but I never gave in. I always tried to remain positive and strong and lived the best way I could, I earned respect and gave respect, even to those who didn't always deserve it and although it always seemed to be a constant battle to live up to societies "expectations", I did my best. Never did I dream of a time like this, where I would be living under constant fear, too afraid to trust anyone. Call it what you like – fear, embarrassment, self-pity – it matters not, I am burdened by it; and constantly battle against becoming a total recluse because of it. So, the battle is not just with those who oppose me but with my own inner weaknesses. I think back to the time when I was a teenager and lived at home with my mother, it wasn't easy trying to re-establish a mother and daughter relationship after spending so many years in a care home, being abused in either one way or the other, but I tried, and I tried hard! Before I built a close bond with her we didn't speak much about past events, but I often sat by her side hoping she would reach out to me, just enough to let me know that she still loved me, but she never did, not until Good Friday, four days before she died. Now I sit and wonder if she ever thought about me like I sit and think about my children; did she ever wonder why it all went so horribly wrong?

It wasn't until I began to understand more about my own mental health problems and what caused them that I noticed that some men obtained vulnerable females as their partners, so they could take control of their bank cards and their state benefits. Drugs, alcohol, cars and recreation replaced food, clothing and personal belongings, this happened to me for years; up until I confided in my counsellor, Clive Powell. It was only then that I took on the role some people portrayed of me and tried to obtain proof of the way I was being treated. It seemed I succumbed to certain individuals and relied upon my counsellor's support and understanding to educate me about those who took advantage of me. Although I have left many unnamed, their abusive treatment towards me seemed to lessen when I was seeing my counsellor and was able to function better. After putting up with years of abusive behaviour that I failed to understand, I found myself speaking to the Lincolnshire police, psychologists and a hospital psychiatrist but it seemed I had not got enough proof to receive their authoritative help or support so, basically, I was on my own. When I think back to the evening of December 19th 2014, when my youngest daughter phoned 101 and spoke to the emergency team about my health condition, I almost gave up my fight to prove I was just a normal human being, reacting in a perfectly normal way to situations that even the strongest of us could not deal with. But once again my survival instincts kicked in and I put up yet another fight to prove that I was as sane as the next person and probably the most level-headed person around here. After being driven to the hospital, my daughter and I spent the best part of five hours with a female psychiatrist, the conclusion she came to, after listening to varied accounts of what had been happening to me, was that I was being exploited and she showed great concern about my safety, particularly within my own home. She went on to say, I was in a very traumatic state and not strong enough at that point to protect myself from those who had become involved with the exploitation tactics. Not having met me before, she decided to speak with a psychologist who apparently had background history of me dating back a few years but was reluctant to give the psychologists name. After advising me to telephone the police if the abuse continued, she reluctantly allowed me to leave the hospital; opposed to committing me for my own safety. She insisted that I didn't see Peter Senior any more and told me that she was referring me to the social services and to the Stamford resource centre. She went on to say, they may well involve the police and if that was the case they would probably arrange for an officer to visit me and an investigation could be the end result! Of course, I protected the people who were abusing me and the whole thing phased away and nothing was done. Very often I think back to that evening and mull over what that psychiatrist said to me and wonder if I had understood what I was really up against; or even if I was well enough to protect myself once she had released me! I often regretted not accepting the initial protection she offered, as the very same people who had been exploiting me managed to win over my affections and trust before exploiting me even further. Like a syndicate, these people grouped together and became a tough force for me to deal with, in a situation like that the only protection I was offered was a psychiatric ward, where my health would have probably declined anyway. That's not what should have happened! What should have happened was staring us all in the face and yet again it seemed "The Innocent" become "The Guilty" and suffered the consequences. I asked myself, "Where does it say in our book of laws that an innocent person shall be committed to a psychiatric ward if they cannot protect themselves against those who intentionally set out to harm them?" Surely it should be the abusers who are reprimanded for the crimes they commit; not the abused!

I consider it all too easy to single people out and have them committed. Certain authoritative individuals find it beyond their intellectual scientific level to understand what the real problem is; if they could listen more attentively and clear their minds of all the other patients they have previously seen and characterised they might see each person as an individual; it is not naivety or irrational thinking, nor is it insanity or psychosis, it is not the fact I suffer from epilepsy or anxiety/depression; it is simply that I am slowly being stripped of my dignity. Being shown very little or no respect from those I have to live near, who amalgamate and become stronger in numbers. So, with very few laws to help people in circumstances such as these, I have very little or no protection. I have no power to stand up to them and no way to eliminate them from my life.

18 December 2014, I recall that I asked my youngest daughter to accompany me to Market Deeping Town Hall to join in with the crowds who traditionally sang carols around the Christmas tree, but when I reminded

her about it in front of Peter Senior he made a deliberate sarcastic remark about her going; just to make her feel uncomfortable. In a town like ours, singing carols around a Christmas tree could be considered an embarrassment to some, most would prefer to get drunk inside the public bars. However, I knew Allishia enjoyed the traditional Christmases and I was really pleased when she said she would still accompany me. For reasons I am not sure about, Peter Senior tried to flout an evening around the Christmas tree with my grandchildren. For a man of his age he was hopelessly inconsiderate as he knew only too well how delicate mine and Allishia's relationship was, after being estranged from her for well over a year, I was trying to rebuild a resemblance of a mother and daughter bond between us but the best advice he could offer me was: be cautious! It was just one more trait that he had in his personality that I could never understand.

Although I wanted people to know about my life, I felt I had very little time left to write everything I wanted them to know. Having had the chance to say very little to anyone, other than the few people directly involved in my life, I was losing hope of ever getting to the bottom of "what was going on". Despite my will and perseverance, I had so many obstacles placed in my path it had proved impossible for me to make a full recovery and I had totally lost all hope of ever getting back to a life of normality.

Over many years I have become totally reliant on Peter Senior and the people he associates with. Any friends I have made have been driven away, either by my typically progressive personality changes and bouts of anger or by Peter Senior's manipulative planning to devi ously control my movements and their way of thinking;

using each one of them as an aid to sustain his control over me.

Marianna from the Stamford Resource Centre telephoned me today but despite her role as a mental health adviser I still feel threatened! Having previously confided in her about my life around Peter Senior, I reeled off only enough to release the heavy burden I felt I was carrying upon my shoulders. Now I feel like I am going to be thrown to the lions. If I don't make sense of the "gaslighting effect" and help her to understand how it has been for me I am afraid I may need that place of safety until such time as we all make sense of this. Like many other victims, I don't possess enough knowledge to describe in the correct medical terms how my health has been affected by all of this, therefore it proves difficult to convince the mental health specialists that Peter Senior and his aides have actually been using what's known as "the gaslighting effect" to worry and burden me. I'm not sure when all this started but certainly before I was well enough to suspect anything. Peter Senior has always very cleverly managed to maintain my trust in him and always insists on giving me what he referred to as "good advice!" What seemed to be the pity was that I trusted him wholeheartedly! I haven't seen or heard any positive communication from George since he came down to my home for an overnight stay on Friday 7 August; but I suspect that Peter Senior has some form of contact with him. It seems that George knows my every move and avoids me like the plague and my life seems to evolve around dates, times, places and arrangements that Peter Senior and his girlfriend Kitty make.

As my relationship with George developed, the situation between Peter Senior, his friends and I became unbearably difficult. George still insists he has no contact with any of them, other than I am aware of, but because of the systematic coincidental occurrences I am reluctant to believe him. He has not been able to convince me of his worthiness as each time I try to discuss my concerns with him, he twists and trivializes everything I say, making me look foolish. I particularly notice that when I mention Peter Senior to him, where he originally gave support and sympathy, he now shows no concern at all and has become uninterested in me or my welfare. As time passes I realise I do not fit in with George's strange lifestyle and elusive friendships and now that Peter Senior is living across the road from me with his new partner, and socialising with her family, I constantly look for a way out of here – but even after approaching every authoritative organisation I still can't get away. Every day I wake up wondering how I could escape the circumstances I am in right now, I don't have the finances to buy a property and move away and although I have approached several housing departments, they haven't really been helpful or understanding of my situation and after lengthy telephone conversations with them, they inform me that the law recently changed and all housing rules and regulations changed along with them, therefore leaving them powerless and unable to rehouse me. I get the impression that helping people like me seems too much trouble for some authoritative individuals, as I have spent a large part of my life struggling and arguing my rights, feeling alone and trapped, crying out for help but not knowing which way to turn to obtain it! When I do finally find the direction, I am blocked by someone in power who thinks they have every right to cast someone like me aside and nothing is done about it!

Monday 8 January 2016. The last few months has been a particularly sad time for me, where I have constantly been feeling unsure of myself, wondering when or if George is ever going to contact me again. I have conditioned my mind into accepting it's all over between us and trying to come to terms with the shattered life he has left me with, so I can move forward, but out of the blue he contacts me again in his usual way, via text, asking if we can chat. I know before he speaks what he is going to ask of me, and it's been the same ever since we met in August 2013. I am always at his beck and call and because I am lonely, with a heart of gold I respond in a positive way and allow him to use me for the heavy chores and duties he assigns me to. Our conversations always began with, "Hello, Wurzie!" – (A nickname he gave to me when I was just a young woman) – "How are you?" And then he proceeds to tell me what a mess his home is in; seemingly as an afterthought he says, "Particularly the kitchen!" After inviting people to stay with him at his home he found himself bogged down in utter disarray and filth which he expected me to clean and put right, without it having any effect on me or our relationship. I constantly cleaned up after him and his elusive visitors, and yet I was never invited to his home to meet any of them. There was a noticeable sequence to his life and expectations of me, where he invited me to stay until I had cleaned the place from top to bottom and then he pressured me into leaving when it was time for his elusive friends to take up residence again. His brother Brian stayed every week and he told me other members of his family fitted into the vacant slots that were left, but when he was alone again he called me, so I would clean up the house ready for it to happen all over again.

It had been a while since we had seen or had contact with each other, up until the point of Christmas Eve 2015 when he contacted me and arranged to stay at my home for a day or two over the Christmas period. I got the feeling that whoever he had been spending time with had suddenly made alternative arrangements for Christmas, which left him on his own, so he used me as a last resort; that way he didn't have to spend Christmas all alone. We spent a couple of days together and as usual I pulled out all the stops to give him a good Christmas and invited him to my son's home to spend time with him and the family on Christmas Day, but I sensed all was not well with George, despite the fact he had tried to disguise his yearning to be somewhere else, I knew only too well that his thoughts weren't with me or my family. Despite all, on 29 December he invited me back to his home, but not before mentioning that he hadn't got any money to buy food with. He told me, since he had moved into his new residence he hadn't been able to keep warm, as he couldn't afford to turn the central heating on or indeed heat the hot water and if that wasn't enough he brazenly asked if I could sort through my selection of herbs and spices as he couldn't afford to buy all that he needed to cook meals for his guests. So, on 28 December 2015 I spent much of my time emptying my cupboards, fridge and freezers of food to take to his place; not forgetting a few tea towels, dressing gowns and various other items he said he had disposed of by mistake when he moved from his previous place of residence. But when we arrived at his home on Vernon Road in Chesterfield his attitude towards me changed completely. I assumed he was angry because he was still worrying about the food situation and thought I didn't understand that it had to last him until February 2016, when he said he would receive the next part of his income. I volunteered to take him shopping for the anti-dandruff shampoo and other personal products he was so desperate for, as well as more food to tide him over. I never left him without food, so as far as I was aware he never went hungry! Each time he described his situation to me it reminded me of all the different times he had gotten himself into similar situations back at Howard Drive in Chesterfield during the first few months of us meeting; then again when he moved to Chesterfield Road in Tibshelf where he lived with his mum. It was at that point I realised how gullible I was, but my feelings for him counteracted any doubt I had about him and things would just carry on as they were. The way he portrayed his destitution seemed to trigger a memory in my mind of the situation I and my younger siblings found ourselves in when we were abandoned as children. I even wondered if George, after reading my autobiography *Little Molly* and *Molly II (Am I Who I Should Be?)*, was playing with my emotions, gaining my sympathy knowing I would help to subsidise what he said he could not afford as it always seemed just moments after I had stocked up with supplies he hinted for me to return to my home. So, on 31 December 2015 until the 3 January 2016 he stayed with me, eating most of what I had left in my cupboards. I have never really heard much from him since that date, apart from an aggressive argument or two over the telephone. The last words he said to me were, "I didn't ask you to do it!" At that point I told him he was an ungrateful swine, I knew from that instant that he only came to my place to take advantage of me. I surmised it was going to be the last time I would see him, but when his bills started rolling in and his finances was being drained again he stuck around long enough for me to become suspicious about his loyalty and faithfulness towards me. I had always doubted his word when I asked him if he was being faithful, as he was never where he said he was going, and at times became so elusive, turning up on my door step after weeks and sometimes even months of not contacting me at all, not even a text or a phone call; just leaving me guessing about our future. When he did finally get in touch or answer my calls he said, "Hi, Wurzie! How are you?" As if I shouldn't expect an explanation, so when I asked for one, his frustration would show, and arguments would erupt, and we would both become angry.

After a period of two years I gradually lost the confidence I had worked so hard to regain and although I knew I had to make the decision not to see him again, I found it extremely difficult. I found it almost impossible to remain calm around him and even got to enjoy the periods of time he wasn't around, simply because he bought the worst out in me. I found myself reacting to his lies and the terrible way he treated me, and it became apparent he was turning me into the nervous wreck I used to be. Between them, George and Peter Senior chipped away at my confidence and turned me back into the frightened little mouse I was before I met Clive Powell (the psychologist who had counselled me for all those years). I hadn't seen Clive for several years, but I must admit I really missed having someone to unload to – he had become a friend, a mentor; the only person I had ever really trusted. I have wished so many times that I was still in touch with him, as in many respects he was like a repellent and gave me protection from those who were only too willing to join the many who abused people like me. When I think of Clive Powell, I also think of his lovely partner, Denise, who remained in the background but was only too willing to contribute anything she could towards helping clients to move on with their lives; and for that I have so much respect for her.

I approached my GP, Dr Wilson, and explained to him the best way I could that I had been trying to turn my life around, after all he had been treating me for many years and knew me to be a reasonably rational woman, so when I discussed George, Peter Senior and their associates with him, he listened attentively to everything I had to say and then put my mind at rest. I knew my suspicions were right about them, they created unexplainable situations making me think I was going crazy, and although Dr Wilson assured me that I wasn't, to put my mind at rest he reluctantly referred me to the Stamford Resource Centre one more time, when I was insistent on seeing another psychiatrist. But when I finally received an appointment I was passed from one level of mental health professional to the other, until I was finally transferred to someone who had the authority to make concrete decisions about my state of mind and what action should be taken, if any at all. I recall it was 1 October 2015 when I kept the appointment to see Dr E. Swanston who carried out a lengthy assessment on me, although she referred to it as a "psychiatric review", which was typical of a long, extensive assessment, which I believe was carried out on behalf of a very nice Dr V. Joseph – a Consultant Psychiatrist, whom I recall meeting on only one other occasion prior to that when I had gotten to the stage where I was deeply second-guessing myself and ready to accept George and Peter Senior's unprofessional decision that I may need more help than I thought.

Although seemingly very nice my first impression of Dr Swanston was that she was quite stern, which made me feel very uneasy, a bit like a child sitting in front of her teacher for the very first time. However, I kept good composure and listened to the explanation she gave to me as to why I had been referred to her, as she said it would become more apparent during the large number of questions she had to ask me. In my opinion the questions were designed to probe deep into the mind and personal life of "a mentally disturbed patient", taking into consideration of course, at that particular stage of the assessment she had very little knowledge of me, apart from the general notes she had been given by her junior college. I sat in front of her and tensely positioned myself in one of the chairs opposite to where she sat and tried to look relaxed. As she began to make conversation with me she very confidently explained the procedure of the questions and I did my best to answer everyone one of them as clearly as I could at that time; hoping none of my answers would be misinterpreted. Not having experience of the new system of the large number of questions that she asked, or sufficient knowledge of scientific terms to explain what I thought she meant by each question, I answered in my own simple terms as much about my life as I could. I must admit, I did at times wonder why I was being asked about my childhood when I had spent so many years unloading the whole horrible experience to Clive Powell. It was one of the most difficult assessments I had ever had in my life. My emotions were all over the place, and after being asked about my hobbies and interests, I told her about my books and why I was challenged into writing them; then it opened up a whole lot more to talk about. Before

I left her room, I glanced at my watch and realised I had spent several hours reeling off as much about my life and how I felt about it as I could. At that stage I may as well have been born transparent, I had no feelings, thoughts or experiences that I hadn't had to divulge to someone and despite the heartache it caused each time I spoke about it, I still couldn't see how repeatedly going through my past could help me to change my life around. I was almost fifty-eight years old and still experiencing problems within my relationships. I wasn't prepared to accept I was to blame for the misunderstandings, breakups and violence which occurred in my relationships and although I had deep respect for the professionals who tried to guide me to a better future, I had to accept that there were certain people in this world who dwelled on seemingly weak, abused individuals like myself. While I spent all those years blaming my own inferiority for the suffering I incurred, I realised I wasn't weak or inferior and I didn't really need anyone to believe in me... only myself! After all, if I couldn't love myself, who would?

When I arrived home, I took a shower to relax the tension that had built up around my neck and shoulders while unloading my personal thoughts and sad memories to Dr Swanston, and tried to clear it from my mind once again. It had been a very strange day and although I had spoken so much about my entire life, I still hadn't found the right words to tell her about George and how disappointed I was in him. I felt too embarrassed to tell her how much he used me and took advantage of my finances and my kindness. I felt I had far too much to tell and far too much to accept but at that stage of my relationship I really didn't feel proud, so I kept many things back from her. I was a grown woman and yet I still put up with abuse from men who really did not deserve someone as thoughtful as me.

On 16 October 2015, I received a letter through the post, a white envelope with red letters situated at the top saying 'Private and confidential', yet I noticed that the self-sealing envelope was not stuck down properly and looked like it had previously been opened. As I wasn't expecting anything else, I guessed it might be the written assessment from Dr Swanston that I had been expecting. She had informed me on 1 October 2015 that she would post me a copy of the assessment at the same time she posted my GP Dr Wilson a copy. As I opened it I noticed it was extremely long, several pages based on what I had told her, it was formally presented, and as I read through it I felt an extreme invasion of my personal self and regretted being so open and honest with her as I was so sure someone had opened the letter before it came through my letterbox. I swallowed hard as I began to read it out loud; a habit I had gotten used to while writing my manuscripts. By the time I had read through the whole of the report I noticed a lot of mistakes had been made, particularly regarding dates etc... some parts of the assessment stuck in my mind and although I feel it is totally unnecessary to print all its contents, I refer to what I feel was the most important...

Dear Dr Wilson,

I carried out a psychiatric review of Ms Smith at the Stamford Resource Centre on the 1st October 2015, under the supervision of Dr Joseph.

Ms Smith was referred to us by the, Steps2Change team who had tried to work with her for anxiety management, however, at their first review Ms Smith was very upset and they felt she would not engage well with CBT. They therefore referred her onto us for full psychiatric review.

PRESENTING COMPLAINT/HISTORY OF PRESENTING COMPLAINT

Ms Smith had a very unstable childhood in which she was subjected to sexual abuse and neglect (please see personal history section for more details of this). She was taken into care when she was around 9yr and describes that, in one particular children's home she was kept inside and rarely went out. She describes, since that time, she has felt very fearful of strangers and has struggled to go outside her home.

Ms Smith describes that she becomes very anxious if she contemplates going out, or even looks out of her windows of her home. When anxious, she feels frightened, particularly of strangers and suffers physical symptoms such as being aware of her own heart beating fast, sweaty palms, shakes and her legs feel weak. She says her symptoms stop if she withdraws back into her home and distracts herself. On a good week Ms Smith may go out twice, though on each occasion the experience is not pleasant due to being fearful, and the physical symptoms described above. She tells me she leaves home for doctors appointments etc… otherwise she avoids it. On a bad week Ms Smith will not leave home at all.

Ms Smith tells me she is fearful of strangers because she thinks people will judge her badly. She denies actually being scared of leaving home per se, such that if no one were around, she would go outside with no issues. She tells me the anxiety symptoms she describes are only brought about by the thought/action of going out. She denies getting anxiety symptoms in any other context.

Ms Smith denies being in low mood currently. Apparently if she contemplates her past experiences/current relationships she becomes upset, however, these episodes pass within a few hours; and she describes getting upset like this about once a fortnight. She tells me that her appetite is ok and her sleep is variable; though there has been no recent change to her sleep pattern. Ms Smith denies having any issues with her temper. She describes herself as quiet and placid.

PERSONAL HISTORY

Ms Smith is the 7th of 10 children. She was born in Chesterfield and lived with both parents till around the age of 7yr when her Dad left. She tells me, that for as long as she can remember, back in childhood, she was sexually abused by her brother John Wass who is 10yrs older than her. She describes that the matter eventually came to a head and he was imprisoned for his abuse of her when she was around 6yr. Following this her mother apparently blamed her for the fact that he had abused her. She describes that after her father had left, her mother couldn't cope with 10 children and apparently she left too. The children stole to survive and looked after one another. During this time, Ms Smith's elder brother, John Wass was released from prison and resumed his sexual abuse of her.

The youngest children lived with no adult supervision for around a year when social services eventually picked the situation up, so around the age of 9yr she went into care.

Ms Smith was kept with some of her siblings and moved around between children's homes from the age of 9yr until she was aged14yr. She describes that in one children's home the children rarely went out and she describes her fear of people and strangers and going out was noticeable at that time. She received visits from her Dad while in care but apparently he was physically unwell. She did not have any contact with her mum till age 14yr when she had some trouble in a children's home and was reconnected with her mum. She describes much conflict with her mum following moving in with her.

Ms Smith was so unhappy at her mum's she ran away from home aged 15yr. She took a job as a nanny with a single dad and had a relationship with him which lasted 2.5 years. This relationship ended and Ms Smith moved back in with her mum. She worked on and off at various times, usually in a role to do with her partner of the time. She had her first child at the age of 20yr and secured a council house where she lived alone for a while. Following this she went onto have 3 more children – one when she was aged 25yr and twins when she was around 28yr when she married their father; they were married for 4 years. While in a relationship with Peter Senior she describes suffering from a profound mental and physical breakdown around 15 years ago. During this time she was not capable of functioning in terms of performing most ADLs and Peter became her carer doing all things for her. She describes that she was housebound for almost 10years and during this time her relationship with Peter Senior ended, though he remained her carer. At this time she started to see a therapist, Clive Powell who gradually helped her to get her functioning back.

Ms Smith currently lives in a council house near to Peter Senior and her daughter. She has a great relationship with three of her children; however her relationship with her youngest daughter is very troubled, however in recent years Peter Senior and her youngest daughter have been very close.

Ms Smith is currently writing her third book about her childhood/life. She tells me that she very much enjoys writing and maintains a website about her books. Ms Smith is in a relationship currently with George who lives in Chesterfield; sees him mainly at weekends. They get on well in general though she tells me there is some, conflict between them.

PMH

Ms Smith describes that she has felt leg numbness on and off for many years to varying degrees. At times this stops her mobilising well. She has twice attended for MRI Scans but was unable to tolerate being scanned so she has no explanation or diagnosis to explain these symptoms.

PSYCHIATRIC HISTORY

Approximately 20 years ago Ms Smith describes a physical and mental breakdown that resulted in 3 of her children being taken into care for around a year.

Then around 15 years ago Ms Smith describes having a complete physical and mental breakdown during which time she stopped functioning and going out altogether. She apparently saw psychologists, Sally Welham and then later started to see Clive Powell, who she saw for 9 years in total. Ms Smith tells me that apart from her therapy with Clive Powell she has only been seen by a psychiatrist once, in January 2014; Dr Mbogo who she saw at a medical centre in Bourne. At this time her difficulties with Agoraphobia, depression and anxiety were noted and she was supposed to have follow up following input from integrated team, though it appears this follow up never came about.

FAMILY HISTORY

Ms Smith tells me that 2 of her sisters have depression.

MEDICATION/MEDICATION HISTORY

Ms Smith is allergic to certain antibiotics.
Gaviscon prn
Nizatidine 150mg OD
Lofepramine 70mg BD
Cetirizine 10mg prn
Carbamazepine 400mg OM, 200mg ON
Salbutamol inhaler prn (uses very rarely)

PERSONALITY

Ms Smith describes herself as quiet and placid, she says that she gets on well with people and rarely has conflict with others.

ALCOHOL/DRUGS/SMOKING

Ms Smith is an ex-smoker. She drinks occasionally and denies any drug use.

MENTAL STATE EXAMINATION

Ms Smith is well dressed and kempt. She makes good eye contact, engages well and good rapport is built. Speech is spontaneous and normal in rate and rhythm. Mood is euthymic subjectively and objectively and affect is reactive. There is no evidence of disordered thoughts. Ms Smith does have concerns about her daughter but these concerns seem well founded and rational in nature with no evidence of delusions around this or anything else. No hallucinations elicited. Cognition is grossly intact. Insight is partial.

Ms Smith denies thoughts or intent to self-harm and she tells me that she has never self-harmed in the past.

IMPRESSION (The case and plan were discussed in full with Dr Joseph)

Ms Smith describes a longstanding fear of strangers such as that when she goes out she will experience significant anxiety symptoms. These issues stem well back to childhood and seem resistant to therapy, as she has previously had therapy for well over 9 years with Clive Powell. It is therefore my impression that Ms Smith has anxious avoidant personality traits that give rise to her struggling with anxiety in this context. Certainly, her childhood experiences would have made her vulnerable to developing such personality traits. It is also possible that she describes some elements that would be in keeping with complex PTSD. It sounds as though in the past Ms Smith has suffered with episodes of depression, however, I find no evidence of depression at interview today.

PLAN

We do not need to see Ms Smith again so I will discharge her back into your care.

1. In the future, if Ms Smith's anxiety symptoms worsen, GP can consider increasing Lofepramine.

Yours sincerely
Dr E Swanston.
Dr V Joseph. Consultant Psychiatrist.

Although I appreciated everything Dr Swanston and her colleagues were trying to do for me, I couldn't believe how the much-shortened version of my traumatic life, from birth to the present time, had been so inaccurately written down on three A4 size pieces of paper, and then sent to my GP as part of my medical records. So many important facts and incorrect dates had been logged about my brother's whereabouts, dates of when he came out of prison and resided at our mother's house and what age I was when all of that happened. It would have taken a master's degree to remember all the exact dates, times and events of such a traumatic childhood and incidents that happened over fifty years prior to that assessment! I wasn't sure, at that stage, as to whether the inaccuracies were caused through lack of communication between Dr Swanston and me or because all of this was done under so much pressure in a "one off session" that took all of 3 hours. It was ludicrous to expect me to recall so much about my traumatic childhood and difficult relationships with clarity and complete accuracy while I was being assessed for mental health issues. I don't blame Dr Swanston for the errors that occurred, but I can't help wondering if it is all too easy to rush through a patient's very complex medical history, which is evidently more important to the patient than anyone one else and may, at some time, come to bite them on the backside, especially if the correct information is not logged on to our National Health medical records. I have noticed one very important factor regarding mental health issues – the stigma it still carries. Although some may think otherwise, there are people who treat those with mental health issues as weak and stupid and of course, with far less respect; only half as important as the next person. A patient's vulnerability seems to depict the amount of consideration and respect they receive from other people and their peers and, because of that, I feel we are being discriminated against. I mentioned the writing and publication of my autobiography and made, Dr Swanston aware of the titles of my books and the reasons for me writing them because I wanted her to understand how difficult it was for me to discuss everything that had happened to me during my childhood and my adult life while I was sat in front of her being assessed. I was conscious of her superiority and professionalism and indeed the time we had to discuss things, yet I wanted to try and help her to understand why I had asked my GP Dr Wilson to refer me to her in the first place and more about my reasons for being there; but I found her general list of fifty questions intrusive and belittling!

Although I have never been tested for dyscalculia, ever since I was a small child I have had great difficulty understanding numbers and facts in mathematics. I have always had problems storing figures inside my head, so struggle to remember exacts dates of things that have happened during my life. If I went for a walk on a Wednesday at 11.45 am and a week later someone asked me what day and time I went for that walk, I'm likely to recall the walk but I would struggle remembering the time and day; unless something significant happened during that time. It is something I have been burdened with all my life, even though I have created a coping mechanism where I can occasionally work out simple addition, I use other strategies to master the art of remembering. I suppose if I hadn't worked out a strategy to make it easier for me to live with, it would have proven to have been a more concrete disability than I have allowed it to be. It seems I have mastered a lot of things during my life by working out strategies of my own... When I left the care homes and wanted to read and write correctly, I spent hour upon hour cooped up in a small bedroom at my mother's house, copying the print from books that I initially found totally boring; just to help me through the hard tasks of life. I was so burdened by my inability to store numbers that at the age of fourteen I dedicated some of that time doing simple sums, nothing complex, but by the time I was seventeen I could add and take away; but my knowledge of mathematics did not progress from anything more than a six-year-old could achieve. It's only since I have matured that I realise how much of our lives are controlled by numbers, dates and the knowledge we have of mathematics which seem to affect so much of our lives and what we are able to achieve. Yet many who have the natural ability to do most things do not use it to their full potential!

I am very proud of what I have achieved during my life, it has been difficult and I've had to struggle to get through it, but "I am one of many", I am a "victim"… but I am a fighter! I gained strength in the knowledge that I wasn't alone with all this, that there are hundreds of thousands of abused men, women and children who at some point in their lives acquire the inner strength to stand up with all their confidence and say, "Today is the day I am going to beat this thing, I am determined to turn my life around".

—⁓—

CHAPTER 16

The Missing Ingredient

I gave lots of thought to a particular television pro-gramme that I had recently been told about. Although I had watched the show before, it hadn't been some-thing I felt particularly interested in, but I felt so desper-ate I switched on the television and watched one of the most pertinacious characters I had ever seen on my television screen. At the end of the programme I quickly jotted down the telephone number and e-mail address that was displayed on the television screen, ready to contact them, but I hesitated as all my confidence had been shattered long ago. I paced around the house while I tried to pluck up the courage to make the initial call to speak to someone but looked for an easier option and decided to draft a message and send it to them via their e-mail address; in that way I figured I couldn't chicken out once my message had been sent. Although I was desperate to find help, lots of thoughts and uncertain-ties went through my head and despite the fact I felt so let down by him, as usual much of my concern was for George instead of me. But I desperately wanted to know if he had been lying and cheating his way through our relationship and although I didn't want to believe he could be so cruel, I just needed to know if he was part of the group who had been trying their upmost to convince me that it was all in my head and I was going crazy; or whether he was genuine. I had never let go of the pleasant memories I had of him from my past, he was a good man, in the sense that I didn't feel he would have hurt me or my children. I was only in my twenties then and considered myself a good judge of character, but things had changed, and everything was so different the second time around. I recall years previously when I first met him, my life proved difficult, my brother John Wass was still pursuing and abusing me and the fear I had of him caused me so much anxiety, things just hadn't worked out between me and George and he maintained I broke his heart. I often wondered if he blamed me for ending our relationship and running away from situations I couldn't handle but I had more than myself to think about; my children had always been my priority! I was never really sure what George thought of our breakup as I didn't communicate that well and because of all the pressure I was put under I wasn't sure about anything. George had sworn on the Bible and his family's lives that he hadn't been sleeping with other women, and never forgot to add, with a great deal of emphasis, "or men", but I ignored his remarks and took it only as sarcasm. I was forever wondering about my life and what I could do to guarantee myself a better future but at that particular time I felt my future and my life depended on his honesty. I needed an unbiased person to advise me, but it wasn't the kind of thing I felt comfortable discussing with a psychologist, so I had no one but myself to rely on. I thought, if I could clear away any doubts I had of him we could possibly build a life together and do all the things we had promised each other, but I needed to know that I could trust him, and he hadn't taken any part in the, "gaslighting effects" I had my suspicions about. I needed to know, when he was advising me about Peter Senior and the terrible situations I was telling him about, that he had my best interest at heart and wasn't just trying to cover up any wrong doing or misdemeanours he was creating along the way. I needed to know that he wasn't involved in this masquerade of pretence that seemed to have been going on around me for far too long. I wanted my life back, but he denied every accusation I threw at him and always turned it around on me. He constantly accused me of being unstable and tried to convince me that I was paranoid, so much so that I continually approached my GP who told me I was reacting normally for someone who was being put under so much pressure, he never failed to put my mind at rest; it was because of the empathy and advise from my GP Dr Wilson that I felt able to carry on. I asked Dr Wilson several times to refer me to someone I could talk to in more depth but by the time the appointments came through I had been through hell and back and because I had informed everyone around me of my appointments with a mental health psychologist, their attitudes and behaviour towards me seemed to change from the deceitful, aggressive kind, to the loving and helpful people I once knew; hence I was fooled by their deceptive ways all over again.

I made the mistake of saying very little about George and his actions to anyone other than my so-called friends, Peter Senior and his partner. I suppose in a way I held back much of what I really needed to tell them because I was made to believe it was my imagination and my mind was just working overtime. I was too scared to approach the mental health authorities again, after suffering from bouts of anxiety and depression I knew it would prove difficult getting anyone to believe me; so I contemplated taking them all onto the television show instead.

It's very rare one writes down or keeps notes while suffering abuse, so some of the things I told TJ's assistants seemed totally incredible. It was only when I was in contact with the assistants and worked alongside them, ready to appear on the television, that I realised I wasn't alone with all this. In fact, there were hundreds of thousands of people all suffering from cruelty and abuse of one type or another. I was shocked to find how difficult it was for me to explain that I was being mentally abused by the person I thought I was in love with. Although it took only one person to believe in me, it was finding that one person, as the biggest fear of all was being betrayed by the loved one who was suppressing me.

I fear that sometimes my choice of words does not clearly explain or describe the extent of the cruelty I have suffered, through no fault of my own I am not able to adequately describe everything I have been through, as I am not as academically sound as I would have liked to have been but I am truthful and have never intentionally hurt anyone, not for gain, or for pleasure; which is more than I can say for some.

When I first went into care, at the age of nine I knew so little about the world and how I was supposed to behave. I had not been raised amongst decent people in a normal way and right up to the age of fourteen I had to work and fight for every morsel of food I ever ate and every breath I took. Yet all of this has made me the kind and thoughtful, generous person I am today and even though I sometimes find it difficult to remain decent to those who hurt me, I am very proud of the person I have become!

It took me all but a few minutes to draft up an e-mail to the television studios; I read it out aloud before sending it.

Hello,

I think I'm being a victim of what is termed as, "Gaslighting".

I am desperate to find out if my boyfriend and the people who are supposed to care about me are creating this effect!

I am desperate to find out for sure if it is happening, or is it really inside my head like they keep telling me?

Yours

Rosemarie

I left them my name, age and my phone number, and then pressed Send before I had time to consider the consequences. I sat quiet for a moment looking at the phone I had sent the message on, kind of expecting an immediate response but of course there wasn't one. It was in fact a few days later that I received a call and panicked when I picked up the receiver and realised it was a crew member who worked at the television studios, I was taken back by their pleasantries when I answered the telephone and for a while I really didn't know what to say to them. I listened carefully to what they had to say and in an abbreviated version gave them as many facts about my life as I could and how it had been for me over the last few years. I explained about my extended health problems and why I had the need for a carer, and the fact he was my ex-partner of eighteen years, despite having separated and living apart for almost six years he was the only person equipped with enough knowledge of my medical condition, so remained my carer. I told them about the strange things that had been happening around me and my suspicions of George cheating with first one person then the next ever since we first met and the fact I thought George and Peter Senior had become buddies and regularly contacted one another behind my back, despite giving the impression that they hated each other; it just didn't coincide with their attitudes to one another when they met! I spieled enough off to give them an idea of what had taken place over a two-year period and found them very understanding, as they lent a very sympathetic ear. They ended the call by saying they would get back to me once they had spoken to the producer. When they did call back, it was a nerve wracking moment when they ran through so many questions, it enabled them to get all the facts before deciding whether or not I should appear on their show.

After taking in so much information, they asked me how they could help me and what I would like them to do; it was at that point I told them I would like George and Peter Senior to take a lie detector test to prove I wasn't paranoid and that my thoughts about them were correct. Both men had been so insistent that I was paranoid and unable to think rationally, I needed to prove they were wrong and that over the last couple of years they had been lying to me and everyone else about me; hoping to get me committed to a psychiatric ward, for no other reason but malice. I explained how desperate I was and felt it was my last chance to prove to everyone involved that I was as sane as the next person. I wanted to prove to all those who had been doubting my ability to make decisions, that these two men between them had been creating mayhem, severely attempting to destroy any rational thoughts I had by creating destruction around me. My decision to tell them about the "gaslighting effect" wasn't a decision I took lightly as I had spoken to so many medical officials about the strange things that had been happening around me. Despite the fact I tried to protect George's reputation by keeping his name out of things, I knew at that point none of it would make sense unless I told them everything; that included the way George, Peter Senior and his new friends had been treating me and how they seemed to relish my confusion and mayhem. I knew before I telephoned the studios that it was going to be difficult to get the crew to accept me onto the show as I knew very well that both George and Peter Senior would amalgamate for strength, solely to try and block any progress I made during the telephone conversations between members of the crew, me and them. I was informed by the crew that George initially refused to take a lie detector test because I hadn't asked him to do it; however, I did recall asking him to do a private lie detector test well over a year before. Of course, George emphasised my poor health and tried to convince the crew I wasn't rational enough to be exposed to a studio audience and Peter Senior, when asked about my relationship with George, tried to put doubt in the crew's minds as to whether I was just being paranoid and told them he wasn't convinced about the things I was saying... that was typical of their alliance.

This was the man who was warning me to be careful, he was the one who eventually convinced me that George was definitely up to no good and didn't deserve me. Even while the crew was carrying out their research I sensed Peter Senior was in contact with George behind my back, possibly planning a way out, and they could bring all of this to an end before they were exposed. George tried to frighten me by saying he would be asking the crew to have doctors waiting in the studios – one more attempt to frighten me into thinking they could have me committed to a psychiatric ward if the lie detector test proved that he was telling the truth. Between them, George and Peter Senior had convinced me throughout many years of torment that it might have been possible I had become paranoid, and just maybe the accusations I threw up at them was all in my head; something I had to find out for myself. I became more determined to succeed in all of this when I realised they would do and say anything to wriggle out of it! When I sat down and considered how much doubt they had put into other people's minds about me and even changed my way of thinking! I had suffered far too much mental torture from the pair of them and asked myself… what further harm could they cause? Unlike George, I was prepared to be proven wrong, all the odds were stacked against me and in a strange kind of way I hoped I was, but it was my intuition that told me I was right about them all along and, though both of them were unaware, I had pre-warned the television studio's crew members that I suspected they would amalgamate to build strength on their side – for this I had to laugh as I knew them both far better than they gave me credit for! My biggest obstacle was travelling to the television studios and sitting in front of hundreds of people knowing that when it went out on air there would be thousands of viewers, all with different views and opinions. I was panic struck! It took an overnight stay in the hotel of their choice and hours of waiting and preparing before appearing on the show. I was nervous for two reasons, suffering from agoraphobia and the fear of being amongst crowds of people, I wasn't sure I would pull it off. When it came to the time of going on set I was surprised how well I handled it, the crew were exceptionally kind and considerate and took great care of me; and suddenly there I was face-to-face with the audience, waiting for the results of George's lie detector test. It wasn't something I had ever dreamed of happening but there I was with far more at stake than just proving a man to be a liar; my life and my sanity was at stake! Soon I heard the male compere say, "George, you were asked....

1. Since the start of your relationship with Rose in 2013 have you passionately kissed anyone else?

   Answer: No
   Verdict: You were lying

2. Since the start of your relationship with Rose in 2013 have you had sexual contact with anyone else?

   Answer: No
   Verdict: You were lying

3. Since the start of your relationship with Rose in 2013 have you had sexual intercourse with anyone else?

   Answer: No
   Verdict: You were lying"

Having given me his word only a few days before, I was dumb struck at the outcome, but the only emotion I felt was utter relief, and as the crowd began to boo, I realised I was going home satisfied in the knowledge that I was sane after all!

—⁓—

CHAPTER 17

Time to Reflect

July 12 2017, I finally received the long-awaited phone call informing me that my eldest brother, John Wass, had been given what Paul Butler termed a "Life Sentence". At the age of seventy-three this should, by all accounts, keep him off the streets and away from children and the vulnerable for the rest of his life. I had been waiting to receive justice for over fifty years, after a lifetime of ill health, pain and anguish, I can finally relax.

It all began with a simple message that I received via my *Little Molly* website that said:

Detective Constable Paul Butler 1915, Divisional Headquarters, Beetwell Street, Chesterfield, Derbyshire.

I didn't really understand why a police officer would be messaging me through my website, so allowing a few minutes to lapse I read the first part of the message again as his name did not ring any bells and, as far as I could remember, I hadn't had any contact with the Chesterfield police since around 1992 when I had cause to report my brother John Wass for trying to smother our elderly father with a pillow. So, although those awful memories had never left my mind, I couldn't understand why they would want to contact me now.

The rest of the message was short and straight to the point...

Hi Rose, I am trying to contact you! My name is DC Paul Butler of the Chesterfield Division, Beetwell Street, nothing to worry about but would it be possible for you to contact me on this number?

I don't actually remember how or when I eventually came into contact with him, but I do remember at some point after that speaking to him over my mobile phone, when he asked if it was possible to meet him at the Beetwell Street Police Station the next time I was in Chesterfield. I very briefly told him about occasionally visiting a friend up there, but it was several phone calls later that I finally managed to fit in a visit to discuss the matter he already had in hand. Paul Butler had mentioned that it was a very delicate matter regarding another close relative of mine who had made a complaint regarding our brother, John Wass, but did not divulge what the complaint was about. However, it soon became apparent to me that my childhood abuse was something he needed to talk to me about. As I had already written part one and part two of my autobiography, *Little Molly* and *Molly II (Am I Who I Should Be?)* as part of many years of extensive counselling and therapy, I no longer felt embarrassed or ashamed of the severe abuse I had suffered most of my life; and knew only too well that the officer would not be approaching me if it wasn't necessary for him to do so. I agreed to attend the police station after making him aware of my circumstances, and as he made the time quite flexible it was easy to fit a visit in during my next vacation to Chesterfield. It was a pleasant day when I attended the meeting. Paul Butler met me in the foyer after the officers in charge of the front desk rang through to his office to inform him that I was there. Before meeting him, I remember just for a few moments actually regretting being there and wondered why I had allowed myself to get roped in to family situations such as they were, but the instant Paul Butler walked through the door and shook my hand, he came across so pleasant my nervousness began to fade away and I relaxed. I immediately got the impression I was going to meet a female colleague of his, someone who was working alongside him and had been made aware of my attendance. I was introduced to Lorna Anderson, collar number 14021, a police woman who specialised in interviewing both children and adults when they had been sexually and physically abused. She was someone who played a very important part in obtaining evidence from vulnerable people, many who had been so severely abused that without her it would have proven almost impossible to divulge everything that had happened. Using video statements to ease the process, she worked alongside Paul Butler and me as a "victim", helping me to relax enough to unload my most traumatic and personal experiences of sexual assaults and violence that had been forced upon me; not an easy thing to do. Recalling my traumatic childhood experiences was far from easy but I found it less embarrassing and heart-rending speaking to officers that showed so much empathy. Lorna Anderson and Paul Butler had set up a video room in a very discreet, relaxed house, not too different to my own home. The house was situated on the edge of a very quiet housing estate, not far from the Chesterfield Police Station so I felt more at ease giving them a statement via video, rather than waiting for an

officer to write everything down that I said. The memories I have of that initial meeting with Paul Butler and
Lorna Anderson are pretty vague considering its impor-
tance. I had previously told so many authoritative individuals about the abuse I had suffered throughout my
life, I honestly didn't think it would have the impact
it had on them. I recall it seemed to take me forever
to unload much of the devastating memories of rape
and sodomy I suffered as a young child and the pain
and anguish I suffered as a result of it. As the hours
seemed to slip by I recalled more and more until it got
to the stage where I thought perhaps I was rambling
and making no sense at all, I was very nervous and
felt ashamed of the severity of abuse I had suffered, and
wondered who in their right mind would want to sit in
front of someone like me, listening to a statement of fact
of so much sexual abuse that it would turn any normal
person's stomach inside out. That's when I realised, it
was two very special police officers sitting in front of me
and I could only think that they had been put on this
earth to rescue me of the torment and burden I had been
carrying inside my head for almost a lifetime. I had told
parts of my abusive history to so many people, so many
times, I was sick of hearing it myself; my past was something I had tried to put behind me, I had achieved the
only goal I had in life and published as much of my life
story as I could recall in the first and second part of my
autobiography, *Little Molly* and *Molly II (Am I who I
should be?)*. For reasons I can't truly understand, I felt a
need to reveal the true facts of my sadistic brother, John
Wass, the child abuser, the rapist, the man that severely
abused me and many others throughout his entire life! I
pitied the police woman, Lorna Anderson, for the length

of time she had to sit with me, listening to every grue-some detail I recalled from a childhood that was so full of pain and hurt that even I wondered how I had managed to live through such devastating ordeals; yet there I was telling my story one more time. Lorna Anderson was quietly spoken with a kind of calm around her and I instantly felt at ease with her. Dressed in plain everyday clothes she had a kind manner and came across as a relaxed, down to earth kind of person, so much so that throughout the whole of the time I spent with her I completely forgot about her being a police woman, therefore found it easy to confide in her about the most intimate details of the abuse I had suf-fered. I recall, I unloaded as much as I could, as quickly as I could, without thinking too much of the pain and injuries John Wass had caused me while he molested me, hoping to get it all over and done with in the short-est possible time. But there were hours full of details that I would have preferred to have forgotten but kept on thinking to myself, 'you can do this!' I made the mistake of thinking that once it was out in the open and on video it would be over for me, my contribution to helping the police with their enquiries so to speak, but it didn't end there for me or the police officers. They spent hours with me while I recalled the memories that had taunted my brain and played havoc with every aspect of my life, throughout my life; until I fell silent! I hoped I had revealed enough of my childhood trauma and abuse that they wouldn't have to see me a second time. I was mentally scarred and felt exhausted, all I wanted to do was go home, take a shower, and cry. Paul Butler stopped the tape from recording me from an adjacent room that he sat in the whole time I was giving my

statement…. I had noticed that room was full of con-
trols so complex it was well over my head. I understood
there was a two-way mirror between the rooms which
seemed to be the only thing between us, and although
Paul Butler had shown me how everything worked
I was totally bewildered by it all. Prior to me making the
video statement, Paul Butler and Lorna Anderson had
very little knowledge of the abuse I had suffered,
however he explained to me that he had picked up on
something I had said on tape and needed to speak with
Lorna Anderson before discussing it with me. It came
to light that John Wass had never been charged for the
sexual offences and assaults that he had committed on
me when he was released from prison when I was aged
nine – the night my sibling and I were taken into care
by the Derbyshire County Council, Social Services
Department. John Wass had served three and a half
years in prison for a combination of offences, one that
included a TIC for sexually abusing me the first time
around, prior to him re-offending. The appalling
offences that he had committed on me somehow
managed to be put into a category of TIC (Taken Into
Consideration) alongside a much more trivial offence of
burglary. I don't know how that happened, as I was of
the understanding that he had been charged with the
offence of rape, underage sex with a minor, incest, oral
sex, anal sex and the breaking of my hymen (the mem-
brane partly covering the opening of a girl's vagina
which breaks before puberty or at first occurrence of
sexual intercourse). Child abuse and rape are considered to be much worse and hold a longer prison sentence, but it seemed for the offences he committed on
me he got away lightly. I was six years old when the

police investigated and eventually charged him, but I had been suffering from his vicious attacks for years, so I felt devastated when I learned he had only been charged with sexual assault and various minor charges. Although he went to prison when I was a child I don't consider the police charged him with the correct offences; for the devastating attacks he had performed on me, he should have been given a much harsher sentence! Although it is over fifty years ago I am still haunted by the devastating injuries from the child abuse and sexual attacks he made on me, although I have tried hard to forget the suffering he caused me, it has been impossible!

During the most recent investigations I became a prosecution witness, and his victim again. I hadn't had time to think about the evidence I had given until Paul Butler asked me if I had ever thought about pressing charges for the abuse John Wass had committed on me when I was aged nine. I remembered I had told so many authoritative individuals about the abuse and assaults he had committed on me at different stages of my life, so initially felt reluctant to even contemplate taking action, as throughout many years I had been desperately let down by the social services department, police departments and even solicitors I had approached when I was a young woman and even during times when my children were growing up; begging them for help but without success. But it seemed this very brave and empathetic police officer, Paul Butler, was offering me the chance to finally put to rest the childhood abuse I (little Molly) had suffered; and gave me the chance to seek justice for the never-ending abuse John Wass had inflicted on me. I felt very emotional when I realised, for the first time in fifty years two police officers were willing to spend time gathering information and video evidence to take action against my lifelong abuser, John Wass. I wondered, did these police officers really comprehend how much that meant to me? By the time I had left that house with Paul Butler, I had unloaded as much as I was mentally equipped to do. Remembering such details of the sexual assaults and physical violence he inflicted on me caused my head to pound and my heart to sink, as never before had I divulged such detailed accounts of the revolting acts he had performed on me when I was a small child, yet there I found myself totally confiding in two people I had never met before. Paul Butler drove me back to my friend's bungalow at Old Whittington, the other side of Chesterfield, just a few miles away from the house. He wanted to make sure I was okay after such a traumatic day and made small talk to try and ease my mind regarding the process they had to go through before being able to charge my brother. I guessed it was only the beginning and, although I was sceptical, I hoped with all my heart that this police officer could finally lock this man away and bring an end to all my suffering.

I must admit I had lost all confidence in the police long before Paul Butler contacted me. Even though I really hoped the CPS would sanction the go-ahead for him to work on the case, I had my doubts that anyone was equipped with enough knowledge and experience in this field to put my brother John Wass rightfully where he belonged – behind bars! John Wass had previously denied all accusations I made against him and although the police did speak to him several times during my adult life, he always seemed to be one step ahead of them; hence he never served time for the offences he committed throughout my life. I hoped Paul Butler would be different, not just for me but for the many other victims John Wass had sexually and physically abused; I was hoping for their sakes too! All my life I had been like a human radar, trying to detect where he was, because of him and his sadistic ways I was unable to put down roots and so I suffered, but as a result of my constant house hopping and running from town to town in a bid to stay away from him, my children suffered too. After receiving several phone calls from Paul Butler giving updates on the case, he eventually confirmed that the police had been given the go-ahead to go full out to prosecute John Wass. Paul Butler had already collected so much evidence that I surmised it wouldn't take long to get the case into court, but of course I knew nothing about the phenomenal amounts of work that was put into a case like that! I wanted to help any way I could, but it seemed until Paul Butler had gathered every bit of evidence there wasn't much more I could do. At the beginning of the enquiries I began to wonder if the information I had given was enough to build a case against John Wass, and I must admit I surmised there hadn't been enough evidence either from myself or the other victims and perhaps the case had once again fallen by the wayside. Of course, Paul Butler kept to his word and often, out of the blue, telephoned me and put my mind at ease. It was during one of those conversations that I learned that Paul Butler had interviewed John Wass, but as I expected he denied everything, but of course I hadn't forgotten the past and gave thought to all the times he had been arrested and questioned by the police; never once had he admitted to the crimes he had committed. I remembered the times when he stood in front of me and other members of my family, bragging that he had committed burglaries and took great joy in boasting about assaults he had been arrested for, but for the majority had not been to prison; I was hoping his many years of good luck were about to change and that Paul Butler was an officer who would not be easily fooled. I recall telling Paul Butler that he would have to be a "good cop" to prove John Wass had committed the offences of abuse he had gotten away with so many times. By studying my brother John Wass and his actions as I grew into an adult, I learned he was aware of certain loopholes in our laws that enabled him to commit offences and get away with most of them, but Paul Butler was adamant, if he obtained enough evidence to prove that John Wass had committed the crimes, he would ensure he was bought before the courts. Up to meeting my old psychologist, Clive Powell, I had never trusted anyone in my entire life, but for reasons I could not explain, I trusted Paul Butler. I had lived my whole life in fear of my brother and yet there had never been anything I could do about it, the easiest thing was to suffer in silence, run when the need occurred and hide when he found out where I lived, it was a cat and mouse situation; I ran, and he chased! Sometimes I wondered if there was an easier way out but I guess I was stronger than I thought because taking my own life just did not appeal to me; I could not face the thought of leaving my children alone to be hunted down by this sexual predator, so I did what was right and stuck at life hoping that one day it would all come to an end and we could live in peace. Throughout a three-year investigation of child abuse I realised there was far more to the case than I originally thought, in fact I wasn't surprised to learn that there was several more of his victims, some willing to give statements and attend court and others too frightened to. Despite thinking mine was the only childhood he had ruined, I learned from this that it was nothing that I did that made him abuse me; knowing that was better than anything I could ever have wished for. John Wass sexually assaulted children and adults alike, abused both male and female in all kinds of ways, assaulted the elderly – our father being one of them. John Wass had no limits, he abused and assaulted so many human beings throughout his life and yet, right up to the point of these investigations, none of us, (his victims), had ever been able to ensure safety for ourselves or our children. My books, *Little Molly* and *Molly II (Am I who I should be),* played a big part in the investigation against John Wass as I had given a very detailed account of the sexual abuse I incurred as a child and remember feeling very guilty and concerned for the fact that Paul Butler had to read the books as part of his investigation. Not immune to such detailed accounts of child abuse, he found them heart-breaking and confessed to me that he did in fact find them very difficult to read, I really admired this man, although he was a hunk of a police officer he was not ashamed to admit that they really affected him! As Paul Butler worked hard to bring justice to our lives, doubt occasionally arose in my mind and I wondered if he would ever crack the case and reveal everything John Wass had done throughout his life. John Wass had lived a comfortable carefree life, supported by certain family members and people who knew him, who were willing to turn a blind eye to offences he had committed. It was never a well-kept secret and although most of us admitted being terrified of him, when it came down to it we gained strength in numbers. During the investigations, certain members of my family passed his type of behaviour off as being "normal", something trivial, but I couldn't understand their way of thinking; surely, they knew what was right and what was wrong. When I cast my mind back to my mother's funeral there seemed to be an awful lot of respect for him, most of our older siblings amalgamated around him, as it seemed with both parents deceased, as second in line he stood to gain, but of course, even our mother eventually accepted he was no good and ruled him out of her will. Had it not been for all the hurt and pain he had caused I might have felt sorry for him, but I knew only too well he deserved nothing more. He controlled our family by putting fear into them and our mother knew it, so right at the end when he could no longer hurt her, she punished him! I suppose in a way, what he did to me throughout my life has made me strong as I do not cow down to anyone anymore and although I may have at times seemed weak; I wasn't when strength was needed. It took Paul Butler three long years to obtain evidence and information from most of my family, not an easy task as most of my siblings for one reason or another are "anti-police" so I suppose it made his job much more difficult. What I failed to understand about human behaviour, we all want the police to keep our streets clean of murderers, rapists and paedophiles and yet when they ask for information to contribute towards helping to catch them, many are reluctant to offer information that could be relevant; thank goodness for the ones who have nothing to hide! I repeatedly conveyed to Paul Butler terrible memories of my traumatic childhood, piecing together my recollections of systematic abuse that I had suffered. He spent much of his time searching for medical files, social services reports and police reports of all the previous allegations that were made against John Wass; from as far back as the 1960s when he began to abuse me. With so much running, hiding and flitting around, my medical records from the age of four to twenty-four seemed impossible to trace, which made Paul Butler's job a lot more difficult than it would have been if the National Health Service and the Derbyshire Social Services Department had kept my records safe. Although I was sent back to my mother at the age of fourteen I remained under the care of Derbyshire Social Services Department until I was eighteen – just as the court had ordered. Paul Butler seemed bewildered by the fact that my medical records seemed non-existent for that period of time and asked me if I was aware of this, but of course I wasn't. I hold social services responsible for a lot of what happened to me as a child, they were engaged with our family long before our parents abandoned us, so I regrettably have to admit that they failed me! At that stage of Paul Butler's investigations, I felt everything was going against us but then he asked me to recall all the places I had lived, people who I had lived with and the reason I left. I was saddened by the fact that because of John Wass and his assaults on me, I had always felt too frightened to remain in my home, wherever it was! For every little bit of information I gave to Paul Butler, he worked hard to find legal documents and records to confirm what I had said. He was willing to listen to many hours of the most horrific and indecent sexual assaults that my brother John Wass had forced upon me, the fear he instilled in me and the physical damage he had caused as a result. The mental abuse he caused me was phenomenal, therefore, for many years it proved difficult for me to vocally express the severity it had on my life. He committed indecent assaults and other sexual offences every opportunity he got, knowing he was going to get away with it... and for a total of fifty years he did! Despite spending many years receiving counselling for the abuse I had suffered, it was so complex I rarely volunteered information to the mental health officials and only confided in the most senior ranks who I presumed had the ability to cope with such devastating incidents. So, I felt really lucky when I met Paul Butler, so relieved I could not put into words the emotion I felt when I realised his aim was to give justice to me and other victims who had suffered at the hands of John Wass. The tall stocky police officer, who by all accounts should have been unscarred by the intricate details of severe child abuse, was actually showing anxiety as a lifetime of ill health, pain and anguish that had been caused to so many victims by one of the most sadistic men in Chesterfield was slowly having its effect; and yet he never gave up! As the investigations passed through another year, Paul Butler remained humble, which helped to unite us frightened victims with the very few police officers who displayed tolerance and understanding without making us feel pitiful, they were compassionate and kind but the greatest thing of all; they displayed their willingness to bring John Wass to Justice. Although Paul Butler and his few chosen colleagues portrayed all these qualities, I must admit, at times I just couldn't rid myself of that feeling of doubt; therefore, I remained sceptical throughout the whole thing. I never allowed myself to think too far ahead, I had tried so many times in the past to have John Wass prosecuted for stalking me, committing indecent assault as well as historic child abuse, without success – so although I put all my trust in Paul Butler, I had very little faith in the British system.

As I recalled my past experiences, piece by piece, I slowly withdrew from society and noticed I was going downhill, my nerves had taken a battering and at times I considered pulling out; as my fear of John Wass was so great I wondered if I was strong enough to go through with it. Over many years of extensive counselling I was gradually able to leave my home and communicate with friends who I hadn't seen for years, but I found the pressure of all the questions and answers very debilitating. I knew from the beginning what I would have to go through to obtain justice; but knowing that didn't lessen the impact it had on me. It was a very traumatic time for me and although Paul Butler put protection in place for all us victims; it still put me on edge. John Wass so often threatened me into not telling anyone about the abuse, I was petrified! I kept Paul Butler's calling card close at hand, as I lived a good two hours' drive away from where he was stationed and knew if ever I had to rely on my local police station for help, I was as good as done for. Paul Butler travelled back and forth to my home in Market Deeping with an enormous crate of paperwork, to save me the 89-mile journey to Chesterfield to update my statements once he had interviewed other victims and potential witnesses. I knew nothing much about his research, only that he was struggling to get any of us to trust him enough to confide in him. I knew he would struggle to gain the trust of my family, as we had been through so much we trusted no one. Despite feeling let down by the authorities throughout my life, I appreciated the fact they had done a certain amount of good and I had long since been aware, if it hadn't been for certain members of the police force, I would have been in a worse situation than I was. I considered the case against John Wass, probably one of the most difficult cases Paul Butler had to solve, and I wondered all the way through it; did he really know what he had taken on? Our family was like a small-town mafia gang; they knew what had been happening throughout many years of silence but kept it close to their chests. Many feared retribution from John Wass and his closest and others feared what might leak out if they got involved. I knew my family like the back of my hand; being one of the most studious I rarely got involved and kept any contact I had with them to a minimum. On occasions I was sought after solely to support and take care of them, even as a young woman I was expected to solve any problems that occurred between them and their spouses and often opened up my home to care for many of my siblings and their children; preventing some of them going into care! Only recently one of the children I had taken into my home when she was around seven revealed she still remembered staying with me, alongside her younger siblings, aged five and three, and of course their mum, who had a long history of severe mental health problems so was unable to take care of herself or her children. Although I was being investigated for epilepsy and seeing a neurologist at the time,

I took them in and cared for them alongside my own children; totalling seven. I hadn't taken on board that my health was worse than their mum's at the time, until I sought medical assistance for her, but because no other member of my family was willing or able to take care of them, I felt there was no alternative and just did the best I could. I knew how difficult it would be to stay on top of things, but they were part of my family and deserved all the love and care I could give them. I experienced many things with my family, caring for their children whenever the time arose was a big part of it. I hadn't really got over the birth of my first born, Ian, before Chesterfield Social Services Department approached me to ask if I could care for three children whose mother was having problems. Apart from caring for my younger siblings when I was a child, it was my first experience as an adult of caring for so many children all at once; children that belong to my family. From that moment on they came to live or stay with me intermittently throughout their lives and, although I was always willing to take them in and treat them as my own, there came a time in my life when I realised I may have made a rod for my own back, so to speak, as in time, within a period of fifteen years I had taken in and cared for six of my family's children, solely to avoid the social services department applying for "A Place Of Safety Order" or Care Orders. I was never advised about child maintenance or contribution towards their food, clothes or any other expense that occurred while I was caring for them. I was a one-parent family struggling to survive, but as far as I recall the children were happy! Unfortunately for some of them, history repeated itself and on the odd occasion when they grew up, I was asked to take care of their children too and the process began again. I helped them because I wanted the parents to pick themselves up and move forward, to create a decent environment and stability within their own homes for their own children, I realised how difficult it was to raise children as I had been looking after children, on and off, all my life so I never forgot how difficult it was. I recall when my eldest niece, Mandy, came to stay with me, since the birth of her daughter Charlene she had been given the keys to her first council property, a two bedroomed terraced house in the centre of, Staveley, a small mining village on the outskirts of Chesterfield in Derbyshire. For whatever reason she had become estranged from her mother and faced raising her child on her own, Charlie was a nickname I gave to Mandy's baby Charlene, and although I didn't intend for the nickname to stick, it did! It was an awfully cold night when I first met Charlene, she was an extremely long baby and looked very pale, not at all like my big bonny twins who were born just months before. It had been snowing as it was so close to Christmas and I was collecting my daughter Cheniel from Nigel who lived in a small flat close to Mandy, in the same town. Nigel at that time only had access to Cheniel, so me and my husband Pud arranged to collect her and visit Mandy on our way through. When Mandy first opened the door of her new home and invited us inside, she looked sad and lonely, different to what I'd expected. As I walked through her house I noticed there was no fire in the hearth and very few pieces of furniture dotted around the rooms, her baby looked cold and hungry and Mandy told me she was struggling to feed her, she had already spent several nights sat up with her, so had very little sleep herself; she looked absolutely drained. If my memory serves me right, it was at that point that Pud went to a local supplier and purchased a bag of coal and firelighters so we could warm up the house. I don't recall having our babies with us that evening so it's possible that Grandma Marshall was babysitting back home in Mansfield Woodhouse; where we lived as a family at that time. Although he lit the fire and purchased food essentials for her, I suddenly realised there were no wrapped presents or a Christmas tree displayed. When I asked what her plans were for Christmas she simply said, "I'll give it a miss this year!" This was a child I had once cared for and felt heartbroken for her, she was a single mum with a very bleak future. Her mother Carol had already struggled to raise her through a very tough period of her own life, my mother and I helped Carol where we could but not enough to change Mandy's or her younger siblings' path in life. Like me, they were destined to experience a hard life, so I felt sorry for Mandy, she was facing the most difficult challenge of her life; raising her own child. My husband and I decided to stay a while with Mandy, taking stock of her situation and chatting with her, I didn't like the thought of her spending Christmas alone with a new baby, who was obviously sickening for something, so I made the decision to take them home with us.

Trying to lighten the atmosphere, I told Mandy, "We are all ready for Christmas, the tree and trimmings are up, and all the presents have been wrapped, the twins have more than enough to share with Charlene!" The beauty of having a twin boy and girl a little older than Charlene meant we had enough clothes, toys and essentials to share between the three of them. I also had older children in the house as my daughter Cheniel was around the age of four and my son Ian around the age of nine at that time. When Mandy arrived home with us she did everything she could to settle Charlene down for the night. At first glance under the light, I assumed Charlene was suffering from a cold, having been without sufficient heating Mandy had kept her wrapped in lots of blankets and a shawl, so I assumed she would pick up and all would be well but I noticed that Charlene wouldn't take her feed and at four am when I got out of bed in order to feed the twins, I found Mandy downstairs, still struggling to settle her baby. I quickly changed and bottle fed my daughter, Allishia, and put her back to bed but instead of attending to my son Kyle, I offered to feed Charlene, as she hadn't taken any feed since before they arrived at our house. I was very worried about her and I could see that Mandy was too, I took Charlene from Mandy's arms and gently nursed her for a short while and felt her forehead, she was hot, and I noticed the light above was hurting her eyes. I asked Mandy to turn off the main light in the lounge and put on a small lamp to rest her eyes, then suddenly remembered what my sister Anne and my mother had told me about meningitis when I was fourteen: "If you lay a baby on their back, crossways on your knee and support their head with your left hand then gently let go, a baby should be able to support their own head, apparently it is a baby's natural response!" Without thinking too much about it I quickly performed that action and then repeated it two or three times before I realised Charlene was not supporting her own head. That's when I panicked and thought she could possibly have meningitis, but because I didn't want to upset

Mandy I hesitated for a second or two while I checked to see if Charlene had a rash but as there was nothing much to go on. I told Mandy to run as quickly as she could to the call box situated on the corner of our street. I gave her our doctor's number and said, "Tell him, your aunt thinks your baby has meningitis, and she's very, very sick." I jotted our address down on a scrap of paper and told Mandy to run as fast as she could, she didn't hesitate or ask questions but immediately ran out of the front door and within a few minutes she had returned and, what seemed the shortest time I had ever seen a doctor responded, he entered the front door carrying a bag and a stethoscope wrapped around his neck. I paid particular attention to his striped pyjama bottoms beneath his heavy black coat and felt very guilty about getting him out of bed.

There was a sense of panic about him and it was at that point I feared the worst. In a somewhat abrupt manner he asked, "Who thinks this baby has meningitis?"

"I do!" I reluctantly answered. I was hoping with all my heart that I was wrong but within a few minutes he hurried me off to the call box with a notelet that he had taken from his bag; on it he had scribbled the type of meningitis it was and sent me off to phone 999.

He said, "Tell them the baby has meningitis and it is essential they get here as soon as possible, she only has a fifty-fifty chance of survival."

When I returned, the ambulance was already at the house, one of the paramedics remained inside the ambulance and sat behind the steering wheel waiting on the other who by that time was carrying Charlene swiftly out of the front door, wrapped in her blankets, shortly followed by Mandy. The siren was blasting out and the blue lights flashing and within seconds they were gone. As the doctor fastened his bag and got up to leave, he walked towards me and gently squeezed my arm to show a little empathy and said, "You, my dear, may have just saved that babies life!"

I closed the door behind him as he left, walked back into the lounge, sat down and cried. I don't know what made me call at Mandy's home that night, it was only by chance that I visited her. I had always had this kind of "sixth sense" that told me when something was wrong and I would just turn up on my family's doorstep when they needed me the most, and the truth is I have never given much thought to anything I have done for them in the past until Paul Butler began to investigate the case against my brother, John Wass. It was only then that I was reminded of good deeds that I have done which many have taken for granted and put by the wayside; purpose to forget them. When I sit back and think what may have happened if I had not been there that night, things could have turned out a whole lot differently! By the time I was forty I had done so much good, cared for so many children and always put myself secondary to others, considering the way I had been raised at home and in the care homes, I remained a kind and considerate person, for which my family have never given me credit. It was only during one of Paul Butler's visits to my home to obtain further evidence for the case against John Wass and give me a general update that he jokingly said something like, "You haven't told me everything!" I was surprised and wondered what he was referring to but without leaving me in too much suspense, he went on to discuss some of things I had done for my family and wondered why I had never mentioned anything to him about them, or indeed why I hadn't written about them in my books, *Little Molly* and *Molly II (am I who I should Be?)*. But I figured as a member of the Wass family it was my duty to help all of them as and when I could. Because I had suffered so much hardship and ruination I didn't want any of them to suffer anything like it, so when I took in children and cared for them, I did it out of love; it was always a pleasure! The reason I contributed towards buying food, clothes, shoes and Christmas presents was because I remembered when I and my younger siblings were small, and we went without; I didn't want anyone else to experience that! When I accepted the role of secretary, adviser and speaker and helped with hours of form-filling, telephone calls and meetings, I did it because somehow amongst the terrible upbringing I had, I learnt more etiquette than most; therefore, more equipped to deal with such things! The reason I visited them all in turn, throughout many years, even though at times I was made unwelcome and they seldom returned a visit, it was because our mother asked me to, I suppose because of her own predicament she couldn't and despite what we all thought, she cared; so, I did it for the love of my mother! The reason I didn't write about it in my books was because I took everything in my stride, I had never considered anything I did for them outside the norm, but now I understand 'A Saint could not have done better!'. For a family with so much hatred and mistrust, I was the one who regularly put my life on hold to give other unappreciative members a chance to survive in a world that would have chewed them up and spat them out again had I not been there to protect them. At this moment in time I do not associate with any member of my family as I feel they are no longer worthy of the loyalty I once had for them, I have witnessed each and every one of them physically and verbally tear each other apart to the extent that every extended member of the family, nieces, nephews, husbands and wives became a part of it; a dangerous force to be reckoned with! Giving it just a moment's thought, I can only recall the very few who have been a credit to this family and have always shown me and my children respect, the majority of their extended family grew up knowing me as "Aunty Ree" – I have a lot of love and respect for them! Jade, the daughter of young Christopher comes to mind; she was like a chip off the old block, so to speak! I always thought she was a lot like me; even down to the hoarse voice I have. Lots of memories come flooding back and disrupt my line of thought again… I guess I did the right thing placing my trust in the police one more time. While Paul Butler spent most of his working days interviewing my family and collecting as much of our past history as he could I was particularly impressed when he told me he had managed to track down the retired police officer who had worked on the child abuse case against my brother John Wass when he was arrested for sexually abusing me the first time around, back in the '60s. Paul Butler was like a sniffer dog on heat, following trails of every tiny piece of information he unravelled from witnesses and victims. He searched through legal documents and records that had been thoughtlessly minimised for whatever reason, making his job more difficult. If it hadn't been for, Paul Butler's perseverance to bring the truth to the surface, I am truly convinced that my brother John

Wass would not have been charged for the offences of historic child abuse or sexual assaults he had committed throughout the years. It took a lot of brawn and experience for Paul Butler to challenge my family and approach John Wass for the offences he had committed most of his life, and certainly throughout mine. There is no doubt in my mind that, John Wass was born with an evil streak and it wouldn't have made any difference to him or his victims had he undergone psychiatric treatment. I am convinced he enjoyed the pain and suffering he put us through, so much so that it was the disturbing effects that it had on us, his victims, that gave him the urge to attack again and again. I am convinced nothing would have stopped him!

After three years of investigations and challenges, Paul Butler took John Wass (DOB 20/01/1948) to trial in Derby Crown Court, he was charged and found guilty with Rape x 3, Buggery x 4, Indecent Assault x 5, Exposure x 2, Sexual Assault x 2, and was sentenced to life in prison, to serve a minimum term of nine years, minus 35 days on remand – minimum term is eight years. To be held on the Sex Offender Register indefinitely. The judge considered all the damage; John Wass had caused me and his other victims and said, "There was no doubt in my mind or the jurors that he has committed every attack, indecent assault and molestation he has been charged with; it was a sentence no more than he deserved. He has committed vile attacks of child abuse and rape on children as young as four." For years John Wass stalked the streets and mixed with unsuspecting parents who had young children because they knew no better than to trust him!

For the ruination of so many young lives he had finally been caught; and justice had been served!

When Paul Butler telephoned me to break the news of John Wass's sentence, it took me a few moments to register the information, as it had been almost fifty years from the day I went into care…. Five years before that, when I was only four, John Wass took away my childhood and ruined my life; and for that I could never forgive him! I consider he has got away lightly. I lost count of how many times he had raped me as a small child and for that he now serves a short sentence towards the end of his life. In comparison to my whole life he has lived a relatively good life with very few, if any, achievements. Where one door closed another door opened but for me and the others, life had not been so good!

—⚡—

Denial

You're in denial but how can that be?
The pain you have caused the suffering you bring.
It wasn't enough to bruise and to hurt,
I am begging you to watch and observe.
Tell me, who created a mind so distort
Were you as a young boy, never taught?
Can you not see the harm you have caused?
I want it to cease; have you no remorse?
A lifetime of hell that should have been Heaven,
You child number two and I number seven.
Both to one family, we were bred,
So many times, I have wished I was dead.
But pay heed, at last, I fear you no more,
I have accepted; you are evil, through to the core.
But now I smile, for I have released;
The fear I once had, the hatred has ceased,
You are no longer, my controller, you cannot harm me,
The damage is done; but now I am free.

My respect goes to every official member of The Derby Crown Court and all those who helped me to get through the court case; I could not have done it if it hadn't been for all those who supported me. I would like to apologise to each person who was chosen to make up the jury, listening to victims and witnessing evidence that would make any normal person become seriously unbalanced; I know it was not easy for them!

—◁▩▷—

CHAPTER 18

Definition of Award

Before I met Paul Butler I had considered giving up my home to move into a refuge but the fact I could not take my dog with me made the thought unbearable, so I suffered the consequence of my decision in silence. I had already suffered name-calling and insults over my 'Little Molly' page on Facebook and sometimes it seemed more than I could bear but the situation became worse when I received, photo-shots of my name being slandered throughout Facebook by those who I had only helped and supported in the past. Those who once looked up to me and treated me with respect took the view that my brother John Wass should not have featured in my book *Little Molly*. No consideration was given to the number of years I had suffered as one of his victims or the fact I was only aged four when he started sexually abusing me, instead one of my relatives who had married into our family made it publicly known that she had "laughed her head off" when she read my book. I had created my 'Little Molly' page with abused children in mind, it was for those who needed to speak out about the abuse they had suffered or were still suffering, but within a few days it was literally destroyed by an inconsiderate woman who gave no thought to a victim of child abuse, so I asked myself, what if it had been one of her own children? That I can only wonder! After three years of recalling the heartache, sorrow and horrific abuse I had suffered, I had tried to move on with my life, picking up the pieces one more time, hoping that all those who once doubted me now understood the difficulty I had throughout my life. I hoped, as it had been proven, that family members could finally accept that it had happened and could take a step back and try to see the whole picture, how it was for us; "His Victims". I believe that acceptance of child abuse is the biggest hurdle we all face! I endured the difficulties it created in my own mother, for those who hold no significance in my life, it matters very little to me what they think, as I have gotten passed caring. All I know is that reporting abuse to the police is the right thing to do. Hopefully, all those who have very little knowledge of it will educate themselves and although I realise in some cases it will be difficult to accept – it does happen!

Sunday 30 July 2017, I turn my mind to all the officials I have engaged with over the last three years and I wonder, what happens next?....

Lorna Anderson collar number 14021 and Kate Morrell 3153 (sexual offences liaison officers).

Paul Butler Detective Constable 1915 Public Protection Unit Chesterfield Divisional HQ.

Carolyn Wright (independent sexual violence adviser).

Julie (Outreach) who arranged for certain steps to be taken to protect me and other victims from any confrontation or intimidation that John Wass or any family member who may have attended to sit amongst the public gallery may have caused.

The Judge (recorder).

Mathew Lowe CPS Prosecuting Barrister.

Gillian who organised things within the court house.

So many good people; I cannot remember every single name of those who were put into place to help and support me and the other victims while the investigations of this case was taking place and I suppose the truth is, without them I would not have gotten through it and although I am very grateful for all the help I received from them, I still feel more could have been done in the first place to protect me! Caroline Wright did reasonably well considering, a large amount of detail regarding the case was put into a category of restriction and confidentiality by the police, therefore she wasn't given full details of the case, or made aware of the severity of it.

Paul Butler dealt with a very serious case the best way he could, with the little resources that were available. Although my opinion would normally be "there's always room for improvement" I considered the fact that apart from the few police women, he handled it single-handedly and did a tremendous job. Apart from the last-minute viewing of the video statements I had made earlier on in the case, I considered I had been treated equally and fairly. But after watching the police's edited edition of my video statements, I was a little taken back by the amount of footage I considered relevant that had been removed. Although I understood it was only done to save time during the hearing, I was disappointed to learn that certain parts, where I had been speaking about previous sexual attacks that John Wass had made on me and some emotional outbursts, had been removed because John Wass's barrister did not want the juror's to be swayed by it, but at the end of the film, I noticed that my full address had been carelessly left in big bold lettering for all to see – which Paul Butler had to remove soon after I had seen it. It was at that stage he informed me that he had not had time to view it himself before allowing me to view it. I remember, at that precise moment I felt a little deflated and let down, it was only a day or so away from the hearing and the fear of going to court to face John Wass in the court room was intensified by that; at that stage it would have taken very little for me to have pulled out! I felt some very important parts of the video had been removed to protect John Wass, and although I had received a certain amount of care and protection while the case was being investigated, I did feel that John Wass (The Paedophile) received just as much, if not more, care and protection than his victims did. I was never shown the edited video tapes again before I gave evidence in the court room, so I trusted Paul Butler's word that my address had been removed and I was safe. During John Wass's trial I was only in the court room giving evidence for a short period of time, which I must admit wasn't as bad as I had expected. Screens were positioned leaving adequate room inside the witness stand and the large microphone that I clumsily caught seemed to dominate the space in front of me, but I was out of John Wass's view which at that particular moment seemed to be the most important thing to me. I was terrified of him, and yet I knew if it wasn't for the fact I was willing to go to court and give evidence, he would remain free to commit more offences and destroy more children's lives. I was old enough and wise enough to know that the police could not do it on their own; they relied on victims and witnesses like me to come forward to enable them to prosecute rapists, paedophiles, and abusers, before they could remove them off the streets, away from society. It was something I knew I had to do, to pave the way for our children!

Ever since I was a young girl I wanted to help others who had suffered the same ill fate as me and yet it seemed the most difficult task in the world was for me to get back on my feet again, my whole life seemed to have turned upside down and the mound of letters and paperwork that came through my letter box was unrealistic, but I was advised by authoritative individuals to put it all behind me and move forward – the problem was that putting over fifty years of my life behind me was virtually impossible! The abuse, taunting and stalking was something I had lived with nearly all my life, so I wondered, how did I put my whole life behind me? I might as well have accepted that I never existed, but of course that would mean I had to suppress the few good memories I had; and the fact that in-between all the abuse and suffering I gave birth to my children! After the most devastating time, I did as they said and tried to move forward but it was like trying to begin my life all over again, but with far fewer years to do it in.

I was almost sixty years old, and as I sat and wondered how I could possibly get my life back on track or if I really had the strength to do it one last time, my children came to mind as I realised they were all I had to live for. I regretted the way I had to raise them and how much they had to suffer and, like them, I had wished so many times they had been born in a different time to a different family but then I realised, had that been the case, my children may not have become "The Survivors" they are today. When people refer to me as being a "Survivor" I feel I am accepting the label under false pretences, as I am truly aware by my own experiences that it is actually my children and their children who are the "True Survivors". I am "The Victim" and have always been labelled as such, therefore I feel it unnecessary to be referred to as "A Survivor". However, my children have remained strong throughout and have passed through extreme difficulties, which perhaps others would not have come through so well, therefore in respect of their strength and determination to do well in life they are the "True Survivors". I have always wondered what people really mean when they use the phrase; "Now you can get your life back!" Do they use the term because they know very little of what it would take "to get one's life back" after a lifetime of devastating abuse? I suppose it's better than saying, "Now that your life is totally ruined; where do you go from here?"

When I stop to think about the little time I have left on this earth, I kind of feel sorry for my younger self, despite mulling through life as a victim, trying to make a go of it, I truly feel for the little girl, "Molly"; the abused child who seemed to be the answer to everyone's anger and frustration, while trying to survive the worst sexual abuse and physical violence anyone could suffer, she spent a whole lifetime "trying to get her life back!". My mind drifts back to the time I was seeing my counsellor, Clive Powell, I recall I tried so many times to write a letter to my younger self, without success! As I sit and wonder if I could do it now, I think about all the years I have suffered, all the beatings I have experienced and still, after all of that, I am still strong and unfearing; I survived even the worst of the situations I faced. I now live alone, constantly thinking about all the regrets I have, the education I did not succeed in, relationships that did not work, and challenges I did not participate in; solely because I was too frightened to. Ever since I came out of the care homes I have had problems socialising, and although at the age of fourteen I desperately fought to survive the entire trauma, I saw other human beings as a threat and gradually became what I would describe as "untamed". My unnatural behaviour was noted and recorded, I fought with anyone who hurt or attacked me or my siblings, and survival was my only instinct. As far as I could remember, apart from occasionally attending school at a very young age, I experienced very little secondary socialisation, so when I was eventually signed out of care at the age of eighteen, I had no idea what society expected of me. Life in the care homes was not good, but it was only when I gave birth to my first child, Ian, that I realised that receiving constant beatings and physical violence inside the care homes really wasn't how it should have been! Being an "abused child" I tended to accept cruelty as the norm as I hadn't been taught anything different; for me, being beaten was considered a normal way of life and fighting the attacker off was something I learned to do throughout my whole life. So, when I think about that little girl Molly, I think about her as the child who was never allowed to flourish, I think about her strength and determination and although I still at times struggle to accept that little Molly was me; I thank those who believed in her and tried to bring justice.

After John Wass had been sent to prison, I was contacted by the officials who assumed, just as I did, that after all the years of suffering the trauma of devastating abuse and neglect, the burden of fighting for my rights had come to an end and I would be recompensed for the damage John Wass and the social services had caused me throughout my life, but I was so wrong as I was faced with the same disrespect and rejection from government bodies and organisations that I have always had. If I really wanted to face another long, extended battle, with further upheavals and struggles, I could continue with the never-ending battle I have experienced trying to obtain 'The Award' the law says I am entitled to for being a "victim of child sexual abuse". My application was posted off to The Criminal Injuries Compensation Authority, Alexander Bain House, Atlantic Quay, York Street, Glasgow with a supporting letter from Carolyn Wright, the Independent Sexual Violence Adviser, Spring Lodge, 12 Dean Road Lincoln on the 19 June 2017. Trying to make things easier for me, as she was aware I did not receive an award for the abuse I suffered the first time around and like every other person who was involved in this case, she assumed an award was warranted and came without question; but of course, they were wrong. 'The Award' people speak so freely about is an amount of money awarded to a victim to try and enable them to build something of a resemblance to normal life after devastation, trauma and the mental and physical damage occurred during the time of suffering child molestation, sexual assaults and sexual abuse. However, what they didn't tell us was that there was a criterion that had to be met; every victim is put into a category of eligibility or non-eligibility… Mine was not awarded as it was put into the non- eligibility criteria because of the new law the government brought in to stop victims claiming any award if the sexual abuse happened before 1 October 1979. As I read carefully through the letter I received on the 1 August 2017 from

The Criminal Injuries Compensation Authority, I realised I was destined not to receive the award, as even the social services department in Derbyshire did not inform me when they signed me out of their care that I could have claimed the award up to two years after reaching my eighteenth birthday; as I had also been sexually abused by John Wass prior to my sixth birthday. Assuming that the Derby County Council Social Services Department knew the rules and regulations of the Criminal Injuries Compensation Authority, I hold them totally responsible for neglecting their duty to inform me of such rules... I try to compose myself while I come to terms with rejection one more time and ask myself, when will the government and the authorities realise that their continual rejections of 'The Awards' for victims who have suffered ordeals that many of them cannot even comprehend only adds salt to the wounds. In my opinion they are no better than John Wass, while he has earned himself the title of 'Paedophile', these government bodies have earned themselves the reputation of 'disgrace'! If the beatings, rape and molestation of a child does not qualify for 'The Award' then what does?

A recent bulletin reminds me that the occasional victim passes through the net and achieves the victory of becoming 'a lucky one' who receives an award that is ordered by the courts, but only after fighting their way through a ridiculous amount of red tape designed to make victims 'the losers'. However, I have joined the many victims who have been robbed of their equal right to receive "an Award that was originally put into place by the government to say, we are sorry your life was ruined by an offender!" John Wass broke me and ruined my life from the age of four, the abuse he inflicted upon me and the damage it caused has lasted a lifetime but, "Be patient," they said, "it may take years to work it all out, but justice will prevail". My life and my emotions have been destroyed and I have been patient, but there are so many people I am up against, value who you are they say, but how can we – if they won't value who we are?

—ᴍ—

CHAPTER 19

Iris

Facebook has this uncanny way of connecting us to people we have possibly heard about but have never met, this is how it happened for me when I first heard about Iris. I knew my father had been married before he married my mum, but it was something I had never given much thought to until I began messaging Iris on Facebook, when she told me that I was her aunty and one younger than her. I was amazed that I had actually got a niece older than me but as time moved on and I got to know more about her, I realised she was one very special lady. Apart from having a daughter with the same name, we seemed to have much more in common and although I still suffer from phobias that prevent me from going out and mixing with people, I would very much like to overcome them, so I could have the freedom to leave my home, as and when I would like. I learned many facts about Iris from other people's messages that was displayed on Facebook, but it was a considerable amount of time later that I realised she was fighting cancer. I learned that she was a special needs teacher and had been to university to obtain a degree; all in all, she was the kind of person I would make time for. After making small talk and getting to know who we were related to and how many relatives we had, we became friends but had never actually met. Then out of the blue she asked about my first book, *Little Molly*, and decided to read it. This was when she asked me lots of questions about the book, how long it took me to write it, was it difficult? Then she asked, "Do you think I could write one?" My heart leaped, and I became really excited at that thought; I had been trying so hard to get at least one of my relatives to write about their life, knowing each one of us have a story to tell, but no one seemed interested. When Iris sprung that on me I thought, Yes!!! That was when we began to contact each other a lot more and even though I didn't want to burden her with small talk, I became fascinated with her. I found it strange hearing things about my father's first family and I felt really sad to learn about their hardships. It was difficult for me to believe that when I was nine I had been placed into the care of the local social Services Department and at approximately the same time, Iris was being placed back into the care of her birth mother, Sheila – a member of our family. Before I learned about Iris I considered my life to have been one of the most traumatic, until I recently read the first book Iris wrote: *My Life, My Story* by Iris Edith Madden. On 20 May 2018 I finished reading the book and although I laughed at parts of it, I cried an ocean of tears at the majority. The book brought back lots of memories about our large extended family, for me it was an emotional rollercoaster, tears one minute and laughter the next. I found it exceptionally upsetting to think that there were other members of my family who treated children badly. It seemed parts of our life were similar and, like me, Iris was given a taste of different worlds, so far apart she wondered what had hit her. My father was also her birth mother's father, he named her Sheila, a child from his first marriage. I recall, I saw Sheila only twice during my life and never felt the urge to visit her again, as like Iris describes in her book, their home was no fit place to raise children. I feel I have bonded with Iris, even though we haven't met yet, she is an inspiration and I feel humbled, as just when I thought my life couldn't get any worse, I realise it could have but didn't! Iris is a true warrior, she fought for her life as a child, and again as an adult when she was diagnosed with Acute Myeloid Leukaemia and after that breast cancer... although I would like to write more about her, I feel it is not my story to tell and leave you with the thought that no matter how bad we think things are – life is not so bad after all.

—◇—

CHAPTER 20

Face Everything and Rise

When I was a young girl I told myself, if ever I had children I would do my very best to raise them well; difficult when one hasn't had a normal childhood. However, I regularly ponder through the mass of photographs that I treasure of my children, Ian, Cheniel, Kyle and Allishia, at different stages of their lives. And although some of the memories are difficult to cope with, the photos tell a story of a mother's dedication; as well as the hardship and struggles we suffered as a family.

Last week, 15 January 2017, I and my eldest son Ian enjoyed entertaining my three-year-old grandson while he played with his new "Peppa Pig" kitchen and utensils; a new addition to the mountain of toys he owns already! During a quiet moment after lunch we pondered through the family photos, to remind ourselves of the good times but always remembering the difficult times too; but laughing at the happiness we experienced. When I separate those two emotions I now understand that there were far more happy moments than we realised at the time. My children's childhood was not perfect but now I know it was far better than some people give me credit for… Their Christmas and birthdays were always celebrated with lots of toys, balloons and a tremendous amount of fun; something our family photos cannot hide. But during the many years of being apart I feel my children have forgotten or erased from their memory the many happy times we shared, and sometimes I think they feel bitter that they may not have had the equivalent to a royal upbringing. I myself feel privileged to have experienced such happy times that I had with them. Sifting away the memories of hardship I recall only the moments of bliss with them. No one else can tell the story of the slippery slide I put together with an old hosepipe, a washing up bottle full of diluted liquid to squeeze onto the shoot of their slide to make a fabulous water-shoot, like my children can. They played on that water-shoot throughout the whole of the summer of '93, by the time the summer of '94 came around I had managed to save up to buy a badminton set with two shuttlecocks, that seemed to take their attention away from the water-shoot for a while, but in no time at all Kyle and Allishia had become bored playing badminton so returned to the water-shoot, but Ian became a very good opponent for me, when I had time away from the kitchen. I tried to teach my children as much as I could of what I knew. During my younger days, sport was always something I was good at, so I would like to think I contributed towards my children's ability to play sports well, just as I hope I contributed towards their knowledge of the world; and how they are surviving it! Everyone learns something from someone and as life goes on I realise that, had it not been for me and everything I learned from my own experiences as an abused child, my own children may not have turned out as well as they have! I have lots of questions that I know will never be answered. I am now at an age where I look back over my life and memories are all I have. I realise I no longer have time to plan a future or change what has already taken place, regrets will always be a significant part of my past, that goes without saying and of course will affect the rest of my life; as it will my children's. While my children and I do not discuss my family background, it is safe to say we will survive the traumatic life we have lived. My life had a bearing on theirs, but they will see that my reluctance to discuss any part of it with them kept them safe from internal sadness, heartache and bitterness. I could not bear the fact that my abusive childhood determines the future of my own children's lives and yet, like a slow reacting poison, it has destroyed them completely. There are words unspoken, thoughts hidden, and yet still they have a whole life ahead of them and I, who still suffer in silence, cannot do anything to help them. When I have tried to compare my life to any lives of the people I have met, I find it totally impossible. When I was entering puberty, I had convinced myself that everything that had happened prior to that was long gone in the past, and would not affect me, my future or any children I might have. I had prepared myself for this "normal life" that everyone told me about. What I hadn't been prepared for was a life of so many ups and downs which I would now compare with a huge game of snakes and ladders, where each time I roll the dice I roll an odd number which always results in me sliding down the snakes rather than climbing up the ladders; and like life's struggles, never seemed to end! When I wrote my first book, *Little Molly*, I achieved something that I always thought would have been impossible, but through sheer determination and the support of people who believed in me, I managed to do something that was previously only a pipe dream. Despite the subject and the contents, I felt proud of the fact that against all odds I had at least achieved one thing in my life that would make a mark in this world.

—∞—

Afterword

Many changes have occurred since Peter Senior and I split up and many things have happened, which no doubt we both regret. However, the clocks cannot be turned back and although I will never know for definite who was to blame for the "gaslighting effect" or even if Peter Senior knew that it was causing that effect on me. Sometimes people do the strangest things to others without considering the effect it has on them. Although he and his friends may have only meant it to be 'a little bit of fun' to brighten their lives, it devastated mine to the point where I almost gave up on myself! I bear no malice for anything that happened in or around my house as I know it doesn't help to bear a grudge, so I will put it down to the kind of mistake we all make at times and hope he will put it down on his list of "biggest regrets!" ….

Suffering from anxiety created many setbacks for me, although I defeated the problems that occurred as a result of the breakdowns I had. I tried to live my life as normally as I could, despite the extensive abuse I encountered during my life, it seems I have mastered more than most and achieved what some refer to as "the impossible". I am proud to say, I have not been beaten by any of this and although at times I have felt so let down by those who I should have been able to rely on, I eventually realised that strength does not come from others, it comes from all the hardships we experience throughout our lives! No matter what help and advice I am offered, at the end of the day, I know it was me, as an individual, who developed that inner strength and took control of my life; I found that was the most difficult thing of all! Although I have gone through phases where I just wanted to withdraw from society and pretend the real world did not exist, it was okay for a while as it gave me time to consider everything that had happened to me before moving on, but we all have to make a stand in this world! The life my abuser took from me cannot be replaced by, a simple "Award"! The strength I have gained from it, I have myself to thank for. For every challenge my counsellor Clive Powell set for me when I was at the lowest ebb of my life and the strength it took for me to unload every thought, fear and experience I had ever had; to write the story of my life, *Little Molly, Molly II,* and now my proudest achievement, *Molly III (The Untold Story!).* Despite the hardships and continuing trauma in my life, I can honestly say I have never deliberately let anyone down, and although I was once stripped of my identity, I have never become anyone but the considerate person I was born to be!

There were so many beautiful things and beautiful people I wanted to write about in my books, but I wanted to clear my mind of everything negative that had happened to me during my life; I didn't want any of it to contaminate the good memories that I am about to make when I enter the next stage of my life. I am soon to be sixty years old – and that, my friends, will be "My New Beginning".

—ᴍ—

A Letter to My Younger Self

As I look into the window of my past, I see you hiding beneath the old wooden table that stands in the corner of our front room, huddled up with your tiny arms wrapped around your knees, you are hidden from view; safe for just a moment. I wonder, what could I possibly say that will instil in you your faith in human nature? There is hope, sweetheart, hope for you and for many other children who are suffering like you. The day will come when you are grown; strong enough to fight back. Have the will to move on, when you do you will love with all your heart, give with all your might, and fear nothing. You will live long and in peace. As you sit and twiddle with your toes, I cast protective thoughts towards the memories I have of you and I see your little head bowed, too frightened to raise it, for fear of more hurt. This, my little darling, will pass, it will not last forever, the day will come when you hold your head high and walk out with pride and you will see how beautiful the world really is. You will wander through life, hurt and abused, but you must be strong, it will eventually come to an end, but you will live and experience undisturbed peace; you will control your destiny. By the time you are thirteen you will have the strength to survive anything, as you will have been bruised and battered so much it will govern your whole personality for the rest of your life, it will be your mental attitude and inner strength that will determine your future. As you gradually move forward in life you will meet obstacles that will cause you to retreat into your shell, you will try and hide away but you must avoid doing that; it will only make your life more difficult. Face the world head on, with your shoulders pulled back, and your head raised high; it is confidence that wins the race! There will be times when your mind wanders back into the past, looking back will cause you regret, looking forward will give you opportunities; my advice to you, my little darling, is to leave the past where it belongs, don't look back when you know you shouldn't, it is the bravest thing to keep moving forward; it is the only way!

(This is dedicated to all the children who have been abused, my heart lies with them!)

—〰—